Hamlyn History
PHILOSOPHY

Art director: Keith Martin
Design manager: Bryan Dunn
Design: Martin Topping
Picture research: Helen Fickling
Publishing Director: Laura Bamford
Editors: Adam Ward and Trevor Davies
Production: Mark Walker

First published in Great Britain in 1997
by Hamlyn an imprint of Reed International Books Limited
Michelin House, 81 Fulham Road, London SW3 6RB
and Auckland, Melbourne, Singapore and Toronto

Printed in China

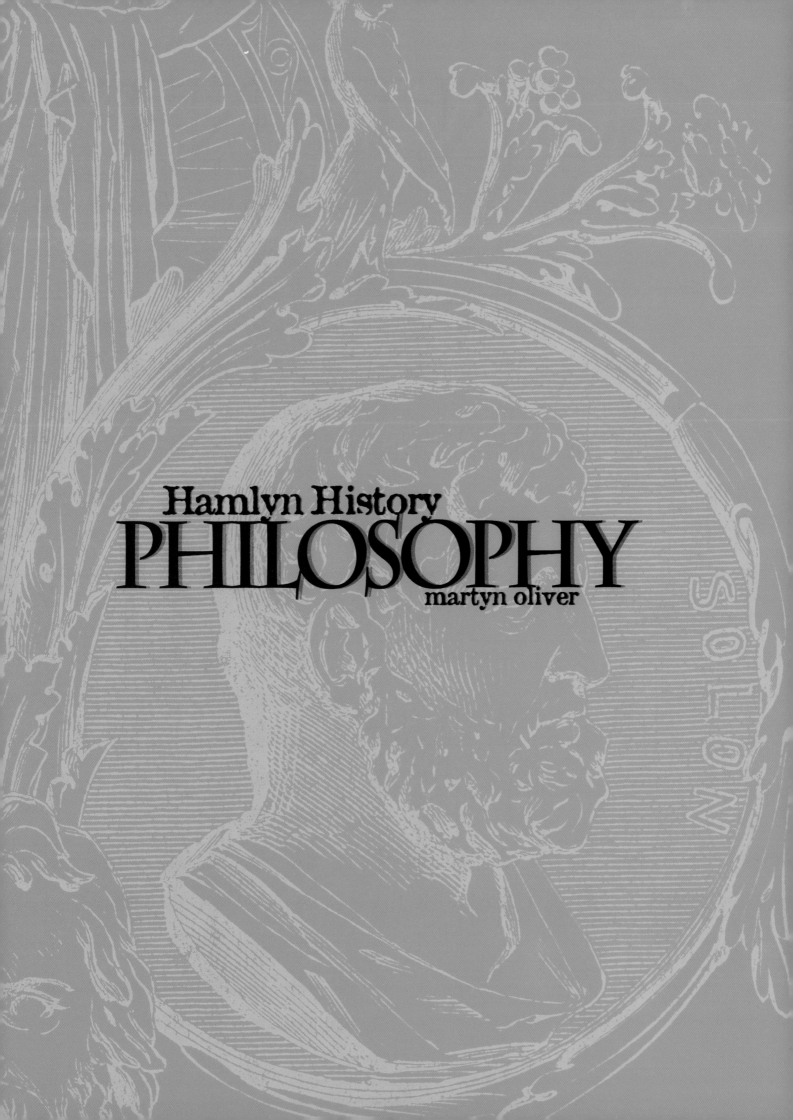

Hamlyn History
PHILOSOPHY
martyn oliver

CONTENTS

CHAPTER SIX
PHILOSOPHY AND REVOLUTION
PAGE 90

CHAPTER SEVEN
COUNTER ENLIGTHENMENT
PAGE 114

CHAPTER EIGHT
SCIENCE AND UTILITY
PAGE 130

CHAPTER NINE
PHILOSOPHY AND
THE MODERN WORLD
PAGE 146

CHAPTER TEN
CHALLENGING AN
ORDERED WORLD
PAGE 170

The discipline of philosophy has never been more under threat than it is today. The success of science in explaining the different facets of human experience has taken from philosophy much of what used to be regarded as its rightful territory. In a world dominated by information technology philosophy would seem to lose out, it doesn't offer its wisdom in small manageable chunks. During the twentieth century countless philosophers have ridiculed their own discipline, arguing that after three thousand years of philosophising, the hope that philosophy could lead us to the truth is an ever more distant fantasy. Yet philosophy is more popular now than it has ever been. Perhaps this is because philosophy is emerging out of the shackles of professionalism under which it sought protection from science and other disciplines for the last two centuries.

Now, what counts as philosophy is less exclusive than it has been for some time. There is a growing appreciation of the deep connections between philosophy and our religious and social inheritance. Few elements of the human experience have escaped the critical gaze of the philosopher. From Plato to Marx and beyond, philosophy has questioned and championed our most cherished beliefs and hopes. It has done so under the premise that our capacity to philosophise is what makes us human – it is what distinguishes us from the animals.

In Ancient Greece, most of what read like speculation on human existence and the natural world counted as philosophy. From the fall of the Roman Empire to the 16th century, European philosophy equalled theology. For most scholars during this period philosophy simply wasn't a legitimate activity unless it presumed the absolute knowledge of God. There were exceptions of course, even among theologians some of whom attempted to carve

INTRODUCTION

greater room for human reflection beyond the all-knowing all-seeing eyes of God. However, from around the late 16th to 17th century, Europe witnessed a growth in scholars who did not assume the absolute knowledge of God. In the late 18th century, in pre-revolutionary France, the group of philosophers who were known simply as the *philosophes* were the focal point for the European Enlightenment. Their celebration of reason and rationality was critical in the emergence of the today's world. In the twentieth century much of philosophy has been dedicated to coming to terms with the modern world, which some believe is now culminating into a postmodern one.

A history of philosophy therefore, gives us a different and more powerful perception of the development of human thought and culture than other histories. Above all, philosophy continues to provide what it has always been renowned for, a special kind of wisdom.

ANCIENT
GREEK
PHILOSOPHY

No other era of philosophy has had such a bearing on so much of Western society. The works of Socrates, Plato and Aristotle have influenced modern politics, ethics, science and culture and their ideas are as hotly debated today as when they were conceived 2,400 years ago.

CHAPTER ONE

CULTURAL REVOLUTION

The Classical era of Greek civilisation, which commenced around 760 B.C., produced many great works of philosophy, literature and science. This explosion of cultural expression was triggered by the use of more sophisticated writing techniques and language. During this period the Greek language, with the use of an alphabet rather than syllabism, could express more complex concepts.

However, while historians emphasise the importance of the development of language, the Greeks themselves regarded the poet

ANCIENT GREEK CIVILISATION

Homer as the forebearer of the new civilisation. Homer's *Iliad* and *The Odyssey* were seen not just as brilliant works of poetry, but as marks of enlightenment that ended the darkness of the 'Archaic' period of Ancient Greek history. Greek schoolchildren were made to learn Homer by heart. His poems depicted the Mycenaean civilisation (approx. 1300 B.C.) which was eventually defeated by the savage imperialism and authoritarianism of the Dorians who dominated until about 800 B.C.

APOTHEOSIS OF HOMER: HIS POETRY BROUGHT GREEK CIVILISATION OUT OF THE DARK AGES AND TOWARDS ENLIGHTENMENT.

THE RISE OF ATHENS

Most of the greatest contributions to Ancient Greek civilisation were made in the fifth and fourth centuries B.C. Significant gains in literature, philosophy and science were made during this period, which began with the emergence of Athens as the dominant in the Aegean area. In 498 B.C. Athens, together with Eritrea, Ionia and Sparta, halted the westward advance of the Persian empire. This victory enhanced Athens' confidence and resulted in the fortification of the city and the establishment of a military and economic league in the Aegean with Athens as the dominant power. Athens now had the prosperity and security it needed for the cultural progress that was to follow.

ATHENIAN DEMOCRACY

The rise of Athens was assisted by the city's unique political environment. For over two centuries the city state of Athens was governed by what is now regarded as democracy in its purest form. It was a political system which followed the original meaning of the word democracy, i.e. rule by the people. All citizens participated in the decision-making process. However, to be recognised as a citizen in Athens was an extremely privileged position.

Out of a total population of about 300,000 only 35,000 people qualified as 'citizens'. Women and slaves were excluded from citizenship as was anyone whose father had not been a citizen. All citizens were members of the Assembly which was the sovereign body of the city state. Assembly business was presented by members of the council. There were 500 people on the council and appointment was by lot. No citizen could serve on the council more than twice, which meant that every citizen served at least once in their lifetime. The greatest testament to Ancient Greek democracy is that, in terms of the degree of participation, it was unmatched in more than 2,000 years thereafter.

SPARTA REIGNS SUPREME

The eventual decline of Athens was marked by war. In 404 Athens finally lost its battle for

Marathon – invading Persians defeated: the dominance of Athens in the 5th century can be traced to its defeat of the Persian empire in 498 B.C.

supremacy in the Aegean to Sparta in the Peloponnesian war. By winning the war, Sparta had inherited the Athenian empire and imposed its authoritarian rule upon Classical Greece which was in the form of an oligarchy known as the Thirty Tyrants. Eventually, the unity of Greek civilisation was broken by the imperialism of Alexander the Great and subsequently the Roman empire. However, while the vitality of Greek culture had been dampened, its spirit managed to filter through to the Roman civilisation which drew heavily upon that of Ancient Greek achievement.

The relationship between mythology and philosophy in Greek thought is a complex and irreducible one. Mythology was a fundamental part of Ancient Greek life and very often the focus for philosophy. Its importance was enhanced by the lack of historical records prior to the emergence of a sophisticated language (c.700–100 B.C.). Thus Greek history and philosophy carried a great deal of myth and mysticism. Although the three great figures of Ancient Greek philosophy – Socrates, Plato and Aristotle – resisted the teachings of the gods, none of them denied the existence of an extra-human authority. Indeed, all three used notions of God's will to justify their philosophical beliefs.

GREEK MYTHOLOGY

OEDIPUS AND THE SPHINX BY INGRES (1780–1867). ARISTOTLE, IN THE *POETICS*, CONSIDERED THE TALE OF OEDIPUS, AS TOLD BY SOPHOCLES IN HIS *THEBAN PLAYS*, TO BE THE PERFECT FORM OF TRAGEDY. MORE RECENTLY, ACADEMICS SUCH AS NIETZSCHE AND FREUD HAVE USED THE TALE TO ILLUSTRATE ASPECTS OF THEIR THINKING.

THE GREEK GODS

The Greeks did not have a religion in the modern sense. Their worship was not governed by fixed creeds; there was no systematic moral doctrine to live by. Greek gods were not incarnations of absolute morality as they often are in today's religions; they were not simply a divine embodiment of good over evil. After Homer's depiction of the gods as having a human form, Greek mysticism became a lot more accessible.

Advice from the gods was used to solve everyday problems and many Greeks would not pursue a public or private interest without first consulting a priest. The gods also represented aspects of life. Dionysus, for instance, was the god of fertility and was widely worshipped. His popularity was in part due to his association with drunkenness and hedonism. He symbolised pre-rational values which were comforting to many Greeks at a time of vigorous rational progress.

PHILOSOPHY VERSUS MYTHOLOGY

The values associated with Greek mythology were comforting to some, but for others they were a hindrance to rational progress. This tension proved a source of philosophical speculation and social conflict in Classical Greece. Most of the prominent Greek philosophers came from aristocratic backgrounds and viewed many of the practices that characterised worship of the gods as backward, barbaric and savage. This attitude is clearly illustrated in the philosophy of Plato, who calls for myth (mythos) to be separated from rational thinking (logos). However, Plato did

"How, then, might we continue one of those opportune falsehoods . . . so as by one noble lie to persuade the rulers themselves, but failing that the rest of the city." from Plato's The Republic, on the usefulness of myth.

use mythology to explain his moral beliefs, which he thought couldn't be expressed adequately in philosophical dialogue. More perplexing, was the fact that much of the conflict between mythology and rationalism was expressed in the form of conflict between different gods. Gods, such as Dionysus and Aphrodite (the god of love), were contrasted with the Olympic gods who represented more sober, practical values.

MYTHOLOGY AND MODERN PHILOSOPHY

Greek mythology has played a surprisingly important part in Western philosophy. Surprising because Greek philosophy partly emerged out of its conflict with mythology. The most famous example of mythology in modern thought is Freud's Oedipus complex which uses the myth of Oedipus (i.e. the son who fell in love with his mother) to describe the complex sexual relationship between parents and child.

Friederich Nietzsche used the myth of Dionysus to appeal to the spirit of irrationalism and hedonism that characterised his vision of the superman. Both Nietzsche and Freud are examples of a recent tendency in Western philosophy to search for an understanding of human experience which is contrary to the Enlightenment glorification of human beings as autonomous rational creatures. This tendency also illustrates how those who favour rationalism against mythology actually use much mythology to explain the reasons for their supporting rationalism. Many philosophers rely upon myths about human nature to support their explanations of human rationality.

TOP: *THE GODDESS ATHENA DISGUISES GOD ULYSSES AS BEGGAR* BY GIUSEPPE MANTUA (1717–84).
ABOVE: THE PSYCHOANALYST SIGMUND FREUD BELIEVED THAT THE TALE OF OEDIPUS ILLUSTRATED SUBCONSCIOUS DRIVES.

Greek philosophy is usually divided into the philosophy which preceded Socrates, and that which succeeded him. For it was Socrates who defended, with his life, the love of wisdom against the teachings of the gods. The philosophers who went before Socrates should not, however, be viewed as insignificant. In fact, recent philosophy has drawn heavily from the pre-Socratics and ensured a revival of interest in their work. The pre-Socratics regarded the world with a curiosity and wonderment which was lost in the more systematic philosophy of Plato and Aristotle.

THE PRE-SOCRATICS

RAPHAEL'S *THE CREATION OF ANIMALS* CAPTURES THE PRE-SOCRATIC CONCERN WITH THE PHYSICAL RATHER THAN THE MENTAL WORLD.

THE EMERGENCE OF GREEK PHILOSOPHY

It is often assumed that philosophy emerged out of a conflict with religion. But this assumption is derived from a particularly modern understanding of philosophy. In Ancient Greece, philosophy emerged out of a sustained curiosity rather than any form of secularism. The area of Ancient Greece which housed the dawning of Greek philosophy was Miletus, a wealthy commercial city in Ionia. The philosophers of Miletus (the Milesian School) were mainly concerned with the physical world and their speculation revolved around the substance or substances which made up the world. Thales, the most famous Milesian philosopher, thought that the world was entirely made up of water, whilst Anaximander believed that air, water and fire constituted the three substances which made up the world. Anaximenes, by contrast, thought that the fundamental substance was air. However rudimentary such beliefs appear to us, it could be argued that they are not dissimilar to Plato's philosophy.

THE PYTHAGOREANS

The most remarkable of the pre-Socratic philosophers was Pythagoras. He is not only regarded as the inventor of mathematics, but also as the creator of an organisation which approximates to an organised religion – the Pythagorean Brotherhood.

According to Pythagoras, '*all things are made up of numbers*'. This obsession with numbers led him to invent several basic propositions in mathematics and geometry which have survived today. The importance of this mathematical work to philosophy is the idea that all general propositions of truth can be derived from self-evident truths, i.e. mathematical ones. This notion has gripped philosophy ever since.

Members of the Pythagorean Brotherhood lived by a strict code. The Brotherhood's rules forbade many acts, including, for instance, the eating of beans and walking on the highway. Much of the religion preached through the Brotherhood is strange even when compared to other ancient religious practices. One of their more accessible beliefs was that order, form and shape are qualities of the good, whilst disorder, darkness and indefiniteness are bad. This view was commonly expressed in Greek mythology which viewed the rationally inexplicable as generally bad.

PARMENIDES:
A WORLD WITH NO STRUCTURE

Of all the pre-Socratics, the philosophy of Parmenides has been of most interest to modern academics. Parmenides regarded

MICHELE TEDESCU'S PAINTING DEPICTS THE PYTHAGOREAN SCHOOL BEING INVADED BY THE SYBARITES. MEMBERS OF THE PYTHAGOREAN BROTHERHOOD LIVED BY A STRICT CODE.

reality as indivisible and infinite. He saw the world as seamless and unbroken and believed that there were no degrees of existence. There could be no permanent structure to the world for this would mean that something existed outside that structure. Therefore, the world had to be absolutely one thing rather than separate interconnected objects. This also meant that change could not occur, because change would contradict the notion of the world as indivisible. Past, present and future were all contained in one.

PYTHAGORAS, THE MOST INFAMOUS OF THE PRE-SOCRATICS, BELIEVED EVERYTHING COULD BE REDUCED TO MATHEMATICAL RELATIONS.

Socrates is undoubtedly the most mysterious of Ancient Greek philosophers. He wrote nothing, preferring to pursue his ideas through public debate and teaching, but despite this lack of documentation, his work has survived to exert a powerful influence over his successors. Philosophy, and in particular the work of Plato and Aristotle, is greatly indebted to him. Socrates, like many great thinkers, suffered for his work, but even when faced with the death sentence he refused to relinquish his beliefs

SOCRATES
(469–399 B.C.)

A TRAGIC LIFE

In 399 B.C., at the age of 70, Socrates was sentenced to death by Athenian judges after being found guilty by a jury for challenging the received doctrines of Athens. His prosecutors said of him: 'Socrates is an evil doer and a curious person, searching into things under the earth and above the heaven; and making the worse appear the better, and teaching all this to others.'

The specific charge against him was refusing to acknowledge the Gods of Athens, but his real crime was his unrelenting passion. For most of his life Socrates survived on a modest income, spending his time voluntarily teaching philosophy and vigorously arguing with other citizens of Athens. Shabbily dressed, eccentric and notoriously ugly, Socrates' indifference to the pleasures and necessities of life was such that he perfectly fitted the archetypal image of the philosopher.

However, his enthusiasm for philosophy also created a number of enemies. One of his favourite techniques for winning over his fellow citizens was to personally embarrass

politicians who claimed superior wisdom by showing just how little knowledge they could muster when questioned. He had little regard for the status of those he questioned. Indeed, he argued that politicians were the chief culprits of intellectual pretence, and that most were intellectually unfit for political responsibilities. This idea was unpopular with those who cherished the democratic values of the city state and it was no great surprise when Socrates was eventually severely punished for his beliefs.

THE IMPORTANCE OF VIRTUE

A close examination of Socrates' philosophy is impossible as there is no original body of work to refer to. We therefore have to depend upon secondary sources. The most reliable source is Plato, who used imaginary dialogues with Socrates as a foil for his own philosophical ideas. It is sometimes difficult to distinguish between the real and the invented Socrates in these dialogues, but what is certain

TOP LEFT: DURING THE TRIAL OF SOCRATES, THE ARGUMENT IN HIS DEFENCE THAT THERE IS NO HIGHER VIRTUE THAN THAT OF WISDOM, MAKES IT A KEY MOMENT IN THE HISTORY OF PHILOSOPHY.

is that Socrates' main concern was with the meaning of virtue.

Socrates' concern with virtue took philosophy in a new direction, because up until then, it had been preoccupied with explaining the physical world. According to Socrates, virtue is a skill like carpentry or shoemaking and the preaching of virtue should only be practised by experts. To be an expert in virtue one needs to be solely concerned with the study of virtuous values. Socrates believed that the citizens who governed Athens were ignorant of virtue. It was this ignorance of virtue which, he argued, led to evil.

THE WISDOM OF KNOWING NOTHING

During his trial, Socrates produced one of his most famous remarks. 'God only is wise; and by his answer he intends to show that the wisdom of men is worth little or nothing . . . He, O men, is the wisest, who, like Socrates,

"Men of Athens, I honour and love you; but I shall obey God rather than you, and while I have life and strength I shall never cease from the practice and teaching of philosophy . . ."

knows that his wisdom is in truth worth nothing.' In other words, Socrates freely admits that he knows nothing but in doing so he claims that he is much the wiser for knowing that he knows nothing. Those people who claim to be wise about matters of human existence are caught in false pretence against the absolute knowledge of God. This in no way implies that the pursuit of knowledge is a futile activity, indeed Socrates believed a life that neglects the virtues of wisdom is completely worthless.

Judged by his own beliefs, Socrates' life was certainly worthwhile but the clearest measure of his legacy lies in the philosophers who were once his disciples.

ABOVE: *THE TRIAL OF SOCRATES*. DESPITE THE IMPENDING DEATH SENTENCE HANGING OVER HIM, SOCRATES REFUSED TO WAVER FROM THE BELIEFS THAT WOULD COST HIM HIS LIFE.

RIGHT: THE MYTHOLOGY THAT SURROUNDS SOCRATES' LIFE MIRRORS THE ANCIENT GREEK PASSION FOR TRAGEDY.

Plato's contribution to Greek thought and the history of philosophy cannot be overestimated. Indeed, it is probably true to say that there has not been another philosopher singularly more influential than Plato. This is mainly because his writings are important not only as great works of philosophy, but also as the founding documents of Western culture.

PLATO (427–347 B.C.)

THE PHILOSOPHER KING

Plato was born in 427 B.C. to one of Athens' most politically influential families and seemed destined for a life of political service in the city state. However, the young Plato was gripped by the impassioned spell of Socrates and decided not to pursue a political career. The execution of his mentor in 399 B.C. left Plato disillusioned with the city state. He felt bitterly aggrieved about Socrates' treatment and he developed a distrust and dislike for politicians.

In his efforts to carry the mantle of Socrates, Plato dedicated his life to philosophy. However, his interest in philosophy was not purely academic and, despite his distrust of politicians, in 387 B.C. he established the Academy – an institution which set out to educate and train politicians. He also attempted, unsuccessfully, to give philosophical guidance to Dionysius I and II, the rulers of Syracuse in Sicily.

PLATO'S COSMOS

Plato was writing during a turbulent period in the history of Athens and so it is no surprise that he regarded the world he lived in as '*in decay*'. According to Plato, the reason for this decay was that the world was: '. . . governed by rulers who do not understand the perfection of things to which that decay is relative.'

Plato believed that the world was made up of objects, which he called *forms* (for example birds or trees) and *ideas* (for example virtue and equality). *Forms* are eternal, changeless and predetermined. They are standards against which things or acts can be assessed for their value. In its purest state, the appreciation of *forms* constituted what Plato understood as knowledge and in Ancient Greece knowledge was equated with virtue. Plato argued that most rulers misunderstood the *forms* of our existence, and thereby lacked virtue; a quality essential for rulers.

Knowledge could be distinguished from mere opinion. For Plato, opinion concerned beautiful things whereas knowledge was about beauty itself. Crucially, opinion was given by the senses (i.e. reason, desire, self-interest), whilst knowledge came from a much higher authority, i.e. some kind of external world.

Justice, according to Plato, was about control-ling the senses because ultimately morality concerned the satisfaction of either reason, desire or self-interest and justice was the attempt to ensure that none controls the other.

THE PLATONIC UTOPIA

The aspect of Plato's work which has remained longest in the public consciousness is his concept of love, i.e. Platonic love. However, the general use of the term is some-what misconceived in relation to Plato's ori-ginal thoughts on the subject and is more rel-evant to his own life. Plato does not insist, philosophically, that relationships be without physical attraction. Instead, he suggests that sexual desire be controlled for the greater good of the whole. This is part of a general idea about the ideal community which Plato sets out in his most famous and influential work, *The Republic* (c.375 B.C.) In the ideal community people's desires and talents must be harnessed for the good of the whole community. For Plato, democracy places the good of the individual above the good of soci-ety. He states that the variety and freedom brought to many in a democracy is wonder-ful in the short run, but, in the long run, is wasteful of the talents available to society. Rulers should therefore be philosophers, or vice versa, so that there is the greatest possible distribution of skill for the good of the whole society. Much of Plato's *The Republic*, which is written in the form of an imaginary dialogue between Socrates and others, con-cerns how the philosopher king might best manipulate the human resources at his dis-posal to create the perfect society.

THE LEGACY OF PLATO

Plato's legacy is so great that it is difficult to find a philosophy that doesn't draw upon his work. Platonic ideas have a powerful presence in the works of the philosophers and teachings of Christianity. His political ideas are, if we account for inevitable anachronisms, still with us, whilst some historians of philosophy believe that Western philosophy has only recently loosened the grip that Plato's ideas have maintained.

ARCADIA BY SANNAZARO – IN PLATO'S UTOPIA, CITIZENS WOULD BE SEPARATED INTO THREE GROUPS: THE GUARDIANS, THE SOLDIERS AND THE COMMON PEOPLE.

Aristotle was the most methodical and systematic of the three great Ancient Greek philosophers. Unlike Socrates and Plato, Aristotle was not driven by a passion to search for justice in the absolute wisdom of philosophy. For Plato, knowledge and justice are inseparable, whereas for Aristotle they are merely intertwined.

Aristotle was born in 384 B.C. at Stagira in Thrace. In 366 B.C., when he was 18, he moved to Athens where he joined Plato's Academy. He remained at the Academy until Plato died in 347 B.C. On leaving the Academy, he travelled to Macedonia where he became a tutor to the young Alexander the Great. Little is known about their relationship and it would be unwise to see Alexander as an incarnation of Aristotle's teachings. Aristotle's most important works were written when he returned to Athens and set up his own school dedicated to teaching philosophy.

ARISTOTLE
(384–322 B.C.)

ABOVE: THE AGORA WAS AT THE HEART OF ATHENIAN DEMOCRACY WHICH WAS CRITICISED BY ARISTOTLE (TOP).

LOGIC

Aristotle's logic, expressed in six of his early works, constitutes a more systematic example of philosophy than any to have been written in almost 2,000 years thereafter. It is far too complex to summarise adequately here, but the main premise involved a theory of semantic structure which Aristotle developed as a framework for understanding the truth of propositions. That framework was essentially a syllogism (i.e. a form of reasoning consisting of two premises and a conclusion). For

example, some temples are in ruins; all ruins are fascinating; so some temples are fascinating. Around this simple structure Aristotle built a complex system of rules of logic which became highly influential, if not dominant, in many areas of human thought until medieval times. It was through the teaching of Aristotle's logic that the primacy of deductive logic was established.

FORM AND SUBSTANCE

Aristotle's metaphysics (i.e. the philosophical understanding of reality) is essentially a modification of Plato's theory of ideas. Indeed, much of it reads like an attempt to tone down the extravagances of Plato, of which there are many. The two most important aspects of Aristotle's metaphysics are the distinction he makes between 'the universal' and that which is merely a particular 'form' or 'substance' and the distinction he makes between the three different substances which make up reality. Each substance has a fundamental essence. The three substances are: 1. the sensible and perishable (i.e. animals and plants); 2. the sensible but not perishable (i.e. man because he has a rational soul); 3. the neither sensible nor perishable (i.e. God). Even though it has carried in various forms into the modern world, this division of substances is distinctly Greek. It is partly a rationalisation of conventional Greek morality, expressed in social and political structures. Consider the table below.

"For as man is the best of all animals when he has reached his full development, so he is the worst of all when divorced from law and justice."

SENSIBLE/PERISHABLE	SENSIBLE, NOT PERISHABLE	HIGHER AUTHORITY
ANIMALS/PLANTS	MAN	GOD
PRIVATE SPHERE	PUBLIC SPHERE	RELIGION/MORALITY
HOUSEHOLD/WOMEN	RATIONAL DEBATE/POLITICS	ABSOLUTE KNOWLEDGE
SLAVES	THE CITIZEN	THE PRIEST

THE POLITICS

In *The Politics*, Aristotle wrote: 'Man by nature is a political animal.' By this he meant that man naturally seeks self-preservation by establishing communities and that the highest form a community can take is a state; the state being the natural result of man's political experience. Women and slaves, how-ever, are the subjects of political deliberation rather than the participants. Aristotle identified three types of state: monarchy, aristocracy and democracy. In some circumstances monarchy is acceptable, but generally he favoured democracy. In Aristotle's democracy politicians, or citizens as he called them, enjoyed a life of leisure. In order to fulfil his function, a citizen needed to be free from everyday concerns that hinder his capacity to think and act in the most rational way. 'Citizens should not lead the life of mechanics or tradesmen, for such a life is ignoble and inimical to virtue.' The economic status of the citizen was to be diverse; it is not necessary for citizens to be rich. The important aspect of their status is political equality. An exclusively rich citizenry would lead to oligarchy. Although Aristotle's idea of democracy is heavily indebted to the practices of the Athenian city state, he was critical of some of its practices. He saw the Polis (Athens' political centre) as too large and potentially detrimental to an efficient democratic state. Aristotle's democracy was by no means a straightforward celebration of liberty – this liberty was countered by equality before the law and by strong intervention by the state in matters of moral significance.

ARISTOTLE'S LEGACY

Like Plato's, Aristotle's legacy is immeasurable and his influence is still evident. The aspect of his philosophy which had the greatest impact on subsequent civilisations is his metaphysics. Until the Middle Ages, Aristotle's logic was the paradigm of scientific teaching and traces of his metaphysics are still found in Catholic theology. In political philosophy Aristotle's account of democracy stands as a foil for the discussion of more contemporary thought.

ARISTOTLE WAS THE TUTOR TO THE YOUNG ALEXANDER THE GREAT, WHO LATER TRANSFORMED CLASSICAL GREEK CIVILISATION WITH HIS ENORMOUS EMPIRE.

GREEK DOUBTERS

Every prolonged period of enlightenment is accompanied by traditionalists, who hanker after times when life was less complicated, and cynics and sceptics who doubt the wisdom of both the new and the old. The Greek Enlightenment was no exception. Very often, sceptical thinking takes hold when the conditions which gave rise to the Enlightenment begin to fragment. This was the case in Ancient Greece. The questioning of the philosophies of the great Athenian thinkers began in earnest when the dominance of the Athenian city state began to decline as it was eclipsed by the empire of Alexander the Great. Two schools of philosophical pessimism – Cynicism and Scepticism – emerged in this period. The latter was to become one of the great schools of thought in Greek philosophy.

CYNICISM

The most famous cynic of Ancient Greece was Diogenes. Indeed, the description of Diogenes as a cynic is where our use of the word originates. 'Cynic' was a Greek word for 'canine' and was used to describe Diogenes because, in rejecting all conventions of dress, food and housing, he lived like a dog. Diogenes lived his own philosophy; everything he owned he carried with him. Ironically, Diogenes' chief concern as a philosopher was human happiness. However, in contrast to his fellow philosophers he believed that humans did not need all of the civilising effects that the great philosophical doctrines thought were necessary for humans to be happy. In fact, he argued such effects were the very source of human misery. For Diogenes, we spend most of our lives chasing objects that are either impossible to obtain, unnecessary or already ours. This kind of self-torture restricts one's freedom of movement and thought. One can

ABOVE: 'DIOGENES OF SINOPE' - THE FOUNDER OF THE GREEK SCHOOL OF CYNICS. DIOGENES SOUGHT TO LEAD A LIFE OF ABSOLUTE VIRTUE, FREE FROM WORLDLY GOODS.

just as easily enjoy the pleasures of life without the effects of civilisation that are regarded as necessities. Diogenes had a similar attitude to the pursuits of his fellow philosophers. He believed that too many of them spent their time resolving problems that were of their own creation.

One of the most famous anecdotes of Ancient Greek thought illustrates Diogenes' attitude. The story tells of an incident where Alexander the Great approached Diogenes to gain his companionship and as an incentive offered him anything he wished. At the time, Diogenes was sunbathing and in response to Alexander's offer simply said, 'Stop blocking my sun.'

SCEPTICISM

Greek Scepticism was not a practical philosophy of life, like Cynicism. Instead it was merely a sceptical philosophical reaction against other schools of thought. The father of Greek Scepticism was Pyrrho whose teachings are dated to the beginning of the third century B.C. According to Pyrrho, the knowledge that was acquired through Plato, Aristotle and others was produced in vain because nobody can ever be certain about one's knowledge of the world. For the Sceptic knowledge of the world consists of statements, but those statements must not be so imbedded in the things they describe that it is impossible to be certain of their truth. Therefore, truth propositions can never be validated; things-in-themselves are separate from our attempts to describe them.

In many ways one can think of Scepticism as Greek philosophy returning, full circle, back to the philosopher who originally gave it its energy, namely Socrates. For it was Socrates who first proclaimed that the wisest are those who know they know nothing. Socrates' enthusiasm for philosophy inspired Plato and Aristotle to create adventurous philosophies and in a sense the Sceptics' project was to repeat his message to their successors.

ABOVE: *ALEXANDER THE GREAT BEFORE THE CORPSE OF DARIUS III, 330 B.C.* CYNICS AND SCEPTICS WERE WRITING AT THE TIME OF ALEXANDER, WHO AMASSED AN EMPIRE WHICH ENDED THE PERIOD OF THE GREEK CITY STATE.
RIGHT: *FAMILY OF DARIUS BEFORE ALEXANDER THE GREAT* – DIOGENES REFUSED TO ADVISE ALEXANDER, WHO WAS THE FORMER PUPIL OF ARISTOTLE.

LEFT: *THE MILL* BY SIR EDWARD BURNE-JONES. THE BOHEMIAN OUTLOOK CAN BE SAID TO HAVE ORIGINATED IN THE FREE-SPIRITED PERSPECTIVES OF THE CYNICS.

وَكَادَ يَنْزِعُ الجِمَالَ السَّيْرُ وَأَنْشَدَ

مَا الحَجُّ سَيْرُكَ تَأْوِيبًا وَإِدْلاجًا وَلا أَعْيَاكَ أَجْمَالا وَأَحْدَاجَا

الحَجُّ أَنْ تَقْصِدَ البَيْتَ الحَرَامَ عَلَى تَحْرِيكَ لَبَّيْكَ الحَجُّ لا تَبْغِي بِهِ جَاجَا

وَتَمْطِي كَأَهْلِ الإِنْصَافِ مُنْفَرِدًا وَدَعْ الهَوَى هَادِيًا وَاجْعَلْ مِنْهَاجَا

EASTERN RELIGION

Religion plays a central role in the history of philosophy. In Eastern civilisations religion and philosophy are almost indistinguishable. The teachings of Siddhartha, Confucius and Lao-Tzu have filtered through to Western culture and Eastern thought has never been more popular.

CHAPTER TWO

The idea of philosophy as a separate discipline from theology and religious teaching is fairly recent. It was not until the 17th century that philosophers thought of themselves as distinct from theologians. Even the Enlightenment did not entirely rid philosophy of its religious and theological connections. The moral and ethical writing of Western philosophers is, in particular, closely linked to Christianity. Philosophy has also always had Messianic qualities which are often represented in accounts of history and Utopianism. Though it is now common to distinguish between philosophy and theology, religion remains a central theme in much philosophy. It is essential to investigate religion and theology to gain a full picture of the history of philosophy.

RELIGION AND PHILOSOPHY

DOES GOD EXIST?

For thousands of years, philosophers have been preoccupied with the question of whether God exists and numerous, apparently non-theological, attempts have been made to prove or disprove the existence of a superior being. René Descartes, widely regarded as the father of the Enlightenment, believed that the idea of an omnipotent power was held so powerfully in people's minds that it must have been placed there by a god. Proof of God's existence was crucial to the foundations of

BUDDHIST MONKS OUTSIDE THE RANGOON TEMPLE IN BURMA. BUDDHISM IS AS MUCH BASED ON PHILOSOPHY AS THEOLOGY.

Descartes' philosophy – which, paradoxically, made one of the greatest contributions to the secularisation of Western thought.

Philosophy's interventions in attempts to prove, or disprove, God's existence are always problematic. It is a question with which philosophers cannot present their views with the conviction reserved for all other philosophical issues. It can be argued that if God exists, no amount of reasoning employed to prove this fact can match his all-knowing status. And, if God doesn't exist, it is futile to argue with those who claim he does exist, because believers will contend that absolute truth is held by God alone. However, this philosophical quandary hasn't prevented philosophers from indulging in speculation about God's existence.

'Philosophy's interventions in attempts to prove, or disprove, God's existence are always problematic. It is a question with which philosophers cannot present their views with the conviction reserved for all other philosophical issues.'

WORLD RELIGION

The question of God's existence is best contemplated with a proper consideration of various of the world's religions, whose traditions also provide an insight into the origins of much moral philosophy. Not all religions believe in a single omnipresent being. Some hold to the existence of several gods and others recognise no god at all. Religions for which the god is not central offer different challenges for philosophers. Buddhism, for example, has explicitly influenced the work of some of the greatest philosophers. Friedrich Nietzsche's idea of eternal return, which conceives of the world as without a beginning or an end, closely resembles the Buddhist and Hinduist belief in a seamless universe, as does his belief in the ultimate futility of any philosophical speculation.

TOP: THE ANCIENT GREEKS HAD MANY GODS, EACH ASSOCIATED WITH A PARTICULAR ASPECT OF LIFE. POSEIDON (TOP) REIGNED OVER THE SEA.
ABOVE: *THE FOURTH DAY OF CREATION* – THE QUESTION OF CREATION IS CENTRAL TO MOST RELIGIONS.

The religion of Buddhism is of particular interest to philosophers. Buddhists do not worship a single omnipresent, all-knowing god like so many religions. Therefore, if all knowledge is not concentrated in a supreme being there is a great deal of room left for metaphysical speculation.

SIDDHARTHA

Buddhism originates from the beliefs of Siddhartha Gotama who, in the sixth century B.C., founded an order of monks which preached and practised his views. He became known as the Buddha (the enlightened one). The beliefs which led him to enlightenment were born out of his despondency with what he regarded as the stale conformity of Hinduism in India. Siddhartha believed

BUDDHISM

progress towards reducing human suffering had been lost in the ritual of mass religion. He proclaimed: 'One thing I teach, suffering and the end of suffering. It is only ill and the ceasing of ill that I proclaim.'

The Buddhist tradition mirrors Siddhartha's despondency with traditional religion and, as a consequence, lacks the normal features of a religion. In Buddhism there is no eternal higher authority for man to look to; just himself. Enlightenment comes from self-reflection and the authority of lived experience. Perhaps the most enduring lesson of lived experience is that one reaches the highest ends through self-subsistence rather than through unrelenting discipline. As the Buddha states: 'Those who, relying upon themselves only, not looking for assistance to anyone besides themselves, it is they who will reach the top-most height.'

THE POISONED
ARROW OF PHILOSOPHY

Although Buddhism is of great interest to philosophers, the Buddhists are mindful of what they perceive as philosophy's limitations. The following parable told by the Buddha reflects this attitude: 'It is as if man were pierced by a poisoned arrow and his friends, companions, or near relations called in a surgeon, but that man should say: I will not have this arrow pulled out until I know, who the man is, that has wounded me: whether he is a noble, a prince, a citizen, or a servant; or: whether he is tall, or short, or of medium

LU-SHE-NA REPRESENTS THE IDEAL ESSENCE OF BUDDHISM ACCORDING TO THE TEACHINGS OF THE PROPHET SIDDHARTHA.

height. Verily, such a man would die, here he could adequately learn all this.' Buddhism is a pragmatic religion. It emphasises action over speculation.

THE SEARCH FOR NIRVANA

The state of mind which Buddhism strives for is called nirvana. This differs from enlightenment as it involves more than just the attainment of knowledge. Nirvana is not a specific set of beliefs about the world because specific world-views decay and become dogmatic. It is a transcendent state where the reality of things is understood and suffering is extinguished. One comes closest to this state when meditating. Despite the indeterminacy of the state of mind called nirvana, the Buddha outlined a guide to the good life. He called this the Eightfold Noble Path.

THE EIGHTFOLD NOBLE PATH

1. *Right ideas*. The foundation of all ideas leading to the noble life are based on understanding the four 'Noble Truths':
i. There is suffering
ii. Suffering is caused by desire
iii. Stop desiring and you will stop suffering
iv. Suffering is reduced by the eightfold path.
2. *Right resolution*. No pain or suffering should be allowed to restrict one's pursuit of the noble path. One must deny everything that is contrary to this goal.
3, *Right speech*. Words can often obscure the truth as it is in one's mind. Therefore one should always be careful to restrict one's speech. In speech one should always seek a middle way between wisdom, respect and kindness.
4. *Right behaviour*. The right behaviour is constituted by the 'Five Precepts'. They are:
i. Not to kill
ii. Not to commit adultery
iii. Honesty
iv. Not to take alcohol or drugs
v. To practise self-control.
5. *Right vocation*. One's vocation must not involve harm to others, either men or animals. It must not involve greed or deceit. One's life must be one of service but it must not involve

responsibilities other than those imposed upon oneself.
6. *Right effort*. One must always express good will towards others, ignore one's own desires and help others to overcome theirs. One must do so with sincerity, perseverance and wisdom.
7. *Right mindfulness*. This stage concerns wisdom. One must always be wary of dogmatism and consider things in relation to their true meaning and significance rather than appearances.
8. *Right dhyana*. One's concentration must always be absolute. If it wavers then one must immediately take action to retrieve it, usually through meditation.

MODERN BUDDHISM

Today Buddhism attracts many followers who, like the Buddha himself, have become disenchanted with mainstream religions. As action-centred, rather than worship-centred, it offers a distinct alternative. Its attraction also lies in the fact that its underlying message is simple: self-control and humility, a message which outweighs commitments to ritual or religious law.

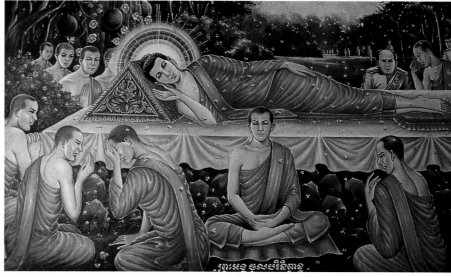

TOP: THERE ARE MANY BRANCHES OF BUDDHISM, FOR SOME THE RITUALS OF WORSHIP ARE IMPORTANT; HOWEVER, BUDDHISM IS GENERALLY MORE CONCERNED WITH THE VIRTUE OF THE RIGHT PATH.

ABOVE: DEATH OF THE BUDDHA FROM A CAMBODIAN TEMPLE. HE TAUGHT THAT LIFE IS AN ETERNAL STRUGGLE CAUSED BY DESIRE.

Hinduism is one of the world's oldest religions – its origin has been traced to around 1,000 years B.C. Many important branches of Greco-European philosophy are substantially present in Hindu thought. Logic, ethics, metaphysics and epistemology all feature strongly and many of the metaphysical debates pre-date Classical Greece.

HINDUISM

THE HINDU TRADITION

Hinduism is not a unified religion. In fact the term Hindu is of European origin. It refers to the oldest known civilisation in India: the Indus civilisation which existed more than 4,000 years ago. Hinduism is made up of a number of India's dominant religious movements, beliefs and traditions and there are six main Hindu schools of thought: *Sãmkhya, Yoga, Mimamsa, Nyãya, Vaishesika* and, the most dominant school of thought, *Vedânta*.

THE CREATION OF THE WORLD

The writings of the *Upanishads* provide the basis for the ancient Hindu philosophy and are held sacred by all branches of the Hindu religion. These sixth-century B.C. writings concern the act of creation. According to Hindu religion, in the beginning all the world was one being. As point ten of the 13 prin-

**"I, indeed, am this creation, for I emmitted it all from myself."
The principles of the Upanishads.**

ciples of the *Upanishads* states: 'Verily, in the beginning this world was Brahma. It knew only itself: "I am Brahma!" Therefore it became the All. Whoever of the Gods became awakened to this, he indeed became it.' Hinduism has just one God, but unlike Christians who believe that God created man and the universe in a single act of creation, Hindus believe that Brahma, the supreme self, transmigrates into all human beings. Brahma is not outside ourselves, it is not above us in the heavens but is eternally our inner selves. To seek goodness therefore we must look inside ourselves, to be at one with Brahma.

REINCARNATION

The highest good man can achieve is enlightenment. This is not to be confused with the Western notion of enlightenment. To achieve Enlightenment one must escape from the circle of reincarnation. Different Hindu traditions have different ideas about how one reaches enlightenment, but generally one's moral conduct must be good as one moves through the circles of reincarnation. One must combine humility and discipline. The principles of the *Upanishads* state that 'those who

are of pleasant conduct here – the prospect is, indeed, that they will enter a pleasant womb, either the womb of a Brahman, or the womb of a Kshatriya (a member of the second of the four main Hindu castes), or the womb of a Vaisya. But those who are of stinking conduct here – the prospect is, indeed, that they will enter a stinking womb, either the womb of a dog, or the womb of a swine, or the womb of an outcast.' In India this belief in reincarnation is central to the caste system and the moral laws which govern it are called the laws of Karma.

THE CASTE SYSTEM

The Indian caste system has been heavily criticised for the restrictions it places on the individual's life chances. It is a system of social class which offers no hope of social mobility: one is born to a caste (class) and dies in that caste. Members of lower castes, most notably the Untouchables, are precluded from much social activity. However, the caste system is not dissimilar to some Western political traditions, for example traditional Conservatism, which also believes in the idea of an organic society in which individuals know their function in society, which must be fulfilled to maintain a well-ordered and peaceful society.

MAHATMA GANDHI (1869–1948)

Hinduism consists of a variety of expressions of religious belief. One of the most powerful expressions of Hinduism was given by Mahatma Gandhi, leader of India's fight for national independence, which was realised in 1949. The foundation of Gandhi's philosophy was *ahimsa* which means non-violence or non-injury. He showed the importance of finding peaceful resolution to conflict and of working to minimalise harm inflicted upon others; learning to endure suffering oneself in order to ensure that injury is not caused to others; having the courage to love one's opponents.

ABOVE: HARE KRISHNAS IN LONDON. THE KRISHNA CULT IS POPULAR THROUGHOUT THE WESTERN WORLD AND TAKES ITS NAME FROM A CELEBRATED HERO OF HINDU MYTHOLOGY WHO IS OFTEN DEPICTED CARRYING A FLUTE. THE MODERN KRISHNAS ARE ALSO ASSOCIATED WITH MUSIC AND ARE COMMONLY SEEN CHANTING IN CITIES THROUGHOUT EUROPE.

THE WAY OF THE KAMI

Shintoism is the worship of the way of the Kami. The way of the Kami is the way of the gods. It is enshrined in all Japanese people and is represented in all great things whether good, bad, beautiful or dreadful. Shintoism, unlike many religions, doesn't have a straightforward set of ethical principles. Instead, Shintoists focus upon the way of the Kami.

People can be close or distant to the way of the Kami and there are two main ways to be in touch with it. The first is through loyalty to Japan, its people and its emperor. The way of the Kami therefore requires disciplined patriotism. By the same token, Shintoism has, in

Shintoism is a religion peculiar to Japan, though it is influenced by Buddhism and Confucianism. Shintoism's association with Japan is so close that the Japanese nation is ascribed a special, divine status. The Shintoist view of creation centres on God's creation of the islands of Japan. According to Shinto scripture, the people of these islands were created a special people with special powers.

SHINTOISM

THE GROUNDS OF THE MAIN SANCTUARY OF THE INNER SHINTO SHRINE AT ISE. SHINTOISM IS A PECULIARLY JAPANESE RELIGION. IT GIVES THE JAPANESE NATION A DIVINE STATUS BECAUSE SHINTOISTS BELIEVE THAT GOD CREATED THE JAPANESE ISLANDS AND GAVE THEM SPECIAL POWERS.

the past (notably c.1850–1945), attached divine status to the Japanese Emperor. The following passage from a 1930s school textbook demonstrates the importance of patriotism to the Shinto religion at a time of intense Japanese nationalism: '...from that time onward generation after generation of Emperors, in a single dynasty unbroken for all ages . . . have flourished in an ever-unbroken line. The successive rulers have without ceasing favoured the nation with benevolent governments and, with reverence be it said, have loved the people just as fond as a mother loves her child.' On 1 January 1946, after defeat in World War II, the Japanese Emperor withdrew

his divine status. However, the love of one's country remains a central theme of Shintoism.

HUMAN PURITY

The other way to remain in touch with the way of the Kami is through the pursuit of human purity. For Shintoists, sincerity is the key to purity. In Shinto this sincerity is called Makato. Makato means much more than just telling the truth, it means a commitment to diligence, integrity, discipline and determination in respect to one's dealings with others. It means preserving one's honour by never failing one's word. Makato also represents a person's relationship to nature, which must be harmonious. Despite this commitment to purity, some interpretations of Shinto suggest that good and evil are relative values. It is circumstance that evaluates an action as good

EMPEROR HIROHITO SALUTES HIS TROOPS AT A PARADE IN 1926. BEFORE THE SECOND WORLD WAR, THE EMPEROR HAD A DIVINE STATUS AS THE LEADER OF THE JAPANESE PEOPLE; HOWEVER, THIS STATUS WAS WITHDRAWN FOLLOWING JAPAN'S DEFEAT IN 1946.

or bad. The circumstances that determine the moral nature of actions are ruled by whether or not they are destructive of the social order of Kami. In other words, whether they are harmful to the communal interest. Generally speaking, the communal interest should be peaceful progress and development. This fundamental ethical principle of the Shinto religion reflects its nature as a religion for which salvation does not involve transcendence. Salvation is always achieved within one's self and one's community.

ISLAM

Muslims believe that Islam is the mother of all religions. According to Islam, the religion's founder (the prophet Muhammad) represented God's final word on earth. The word of Muhammad followed the prophecies of Moses and Jesus in passing on God's final message to humanity. Even more sacred than Muhammad himself is the book he delivered to humanity, the Qur'an (or the Koran), the sacred book of Islam. The Qur'an is Allah's (God's) final word to us.

THE PROPHET MUHAMMAD (570–632)

Muhammad was born in Arabia in A.D. 570. In 610 he was visited by the angel Gabriel in a cave just outside Mecca, where he lived. The angel Gabriel carried a message from Allah which became the *Qur'an*. Mohammed claimed no miracle except for the word of the *Qur'an*. But this was miraculous enough, because the *Qur'an* was written in the most elegant Arabic prose. So elegant, poetic and grammatically perfect that it was considered unlikely to have been by a human being alone. Part of the angel's message requested that Muhammad spread the word of the *Qur'an*. The Arab world within which Mohammed's message was spread was hostile and contained many different religious and mystical practices – most of which believed in many gods rather than just one. However, Mohammed's message was slowly accepted by more and more followers until in A.D. 622 they followed him to a city called Medina. This city, under Muhammad's control, dominated the Arab world and by A.D. 700 the Islamic world had conquered everywhere from Armenia to North Africa and even Spain and parts of France.

THE QUR'AN

The *Qur'an* contains much which is also evident in both Christianity and Judaism. The most obvious similarities are the Islamic acceptance of Moses and Jesus as prophets. However, Islam doesn't accept the idea that Jesus was a divine incarnation. For Islam God does not represent himself in human form, he merely assigns prophets to preach his message. Like the Bible, however, the *Qur'an* teaches that human beings are by nature good. When we do evil we are selfishly forgetting our obligation to Allah who has given us our soul. This means that not all of our actions are divinely ordained by God, a view not shared with Christian theology until recently. But like Christianity, Muslims (followers of Islam) believe that one's actions are judged at our death. This day of reckoning, according to Islam, determines our path to heaven or hell. The *Qur'an* details the moral character of our actions more explicitly than other religions.

The foundation for judging the nature of our actions is the Five Pillars of Islam.

THE FIVE PILLARS OF ISLAM

1. That Allah is the only God and that Muhammad is Allah's final and true Apostle.
2. To offer prayer to Allah (at least five times a day).
3. To be eternally charitable.
4. To perform the pilgrimage to Mecca.
5. To fast during the month of Ramadan.

ISLAM AND THE WEST

The publication of Salman Rushdie's *Satanic Verses* brought one of the most pressing political and philosophical issues of the 20th century into focus. The book reinterpreted the historical figure of Muhammad in a way that deeply offended many Muslims. It painted a picture of Mohammed as a corrupt and shrewd businessman rather than a thoroughly righteous prophet. Rushdie's book so offended the Ayatollah Khomeini, the religious and political leader of Iran, that he issued a fatwa (an instruction to all Muslims to execute a perceived wrongdoer) against him and his publishers wherever they might be. Rushdie's book and the fatwa provoked a fierce debate about the conflict between freedom of speech and religious toleration.

Islam is currently the fastest growing religion in the world and some of its followers have formed fanatical groups which regard the West as inherently evil and thus worthy of punishment. Following the end of the cold war, many in the West have come to regard Islam and particularly the fundamentalist branches of the religion as the chief threat to the West. However, this probably has more to do with the political vacuum caused by the collapse of Communism than any potential threat itself.

Lao-tzu was a contemporary of Confucius, working in the 6th century B.C. Little is known about Lao-tzu's life and even less can be confirmed by historical records. What is known, however, is that he wrote a small book called Tao-te Ching (The Way and its Power) which continues to capture the minds of many Chinese people. The wisdom of Tao-te Ching was spread by a group of disciples who developed a movement which became both a religion and a powerful philosophical school.

LAO-TZU
(604–531 B.C.)

Human beings must follow The Way if they wish to live in harmony with themselves and nature. However, the way of the world cannot be codified or known in any absolute sense. The Way is outside the grasp of reason as it is simply too overwhelming to be captured completely by the human mind. Paradoxically, Taoists believe that one cannot find the true path that is The Way, but that humanity is best served by following it. The central force of Taoism is the way in which it manages to maintain this paradox.

PHILOSOPHICAL TAOISM

Philosophical Taoism is concerned with the best way to live. The central concept in this regard is ch'i, which literally means breath but also describes a particular type of energy. For Taoists a pure form of ch'i runs through all of us. The object of philosophical Taoism is to rid the self of that which pollutes or dampens the ch'i. The chief way in which the ch'i inside ourselves can become blocked is through the expenditure of energy on futile or unnecessary pursuits. In particular those that are driven by vanity. One of the most powerful ways of realising one's ch'i is meditational yoga. During meditation one should extinguish all thoughts of personal ambition and emotion, indeed all distracting thoughts – concentration needs to be total. One's ch'i will never be completely pure but it can be purer as the meditation becomes purer.

RELIGIOUS TAOISM

Religious Taoism's only similarity with other religions is its institutionalisation of places of worship, i.e. the Church of Taoism. Religious Taoism contains much more mysticism than other forms of Taoism. Like philosophical Taoism, religious Taoism is committed to a belief in a fundamental energy which, if used properly, will lead to the right path. However, religious Taoism has a quite different way of reaching this energy. Rather than meditation, religious Taoists favour magic and sorcery. Believers attend the Church to receive remedies for particular ills affecting the sources of their energy.

THE TAOIST WAY
The central doctrine of Taoism is belief in 'The Way'. The Way refers to a way in which the world both ought to be and essentially is.

CONFUCIUS
(551–479 B.C.)

Confucius, or Kung-fu-tse as he is otherwise known, was born in a Chinese state called Lu in 551 B.C. He was a teacher and philosopher, but his maxims and moral values became so influential that Confucianism can almost be regarded as religion. Confucius began his working life as a tutor and his skills drew admirers and disciples, many of whom devoted their lives to him. However, Confucius was unhappy with the society he lived in and set out on a journey to convert the rulers of China to his moral teachings. During a 13-year pilgrimage across China, Confucius tried in vain to convince the rulers whom he met to rule with moral integrity. His attempts to persuade them to allow him to rule in the manner of his ethical teachings also met with failure. However, this did not affect the popularity of his teachings which grew after his death until the Communist Revolution in China.

ABOVE: CONFUCIUS OVERSEES AN EXORCISM OF EVIL INFLUENCES. HE WAS BOTH A PHILOSOPHER AND A TEACHER, BUT NOT A DIVINE PROPHET. HOWEVER, HIS TEACHINGS HAVE ACHIEVED RELIGIOUS STATUS.

THE GREAT TEACHER

Confucius was born into a chaotic China. The Chou Dynasty, which governed China at the time, was slowly deteriorating and being replaced by brutal war-lords. Mass genocide, sometimes on the scale of hundreds of thousands, was commonplace as the usual rituals of war were pushed aside. The main causes of such chaos were due not solely to incompetence on behalf of the Chou rulers. During Confucius's lifetime, the traditions which had until then dominated Chinese society for centuries were becoming weaker and giving way to a more individualist culture. This crisis in Chinese society during the 6th century B.C. was the reason why Confucius's teachings were so powerful.

ETHICAL IDEALS

The foundation of Confucius's teachings are his beliefs about the cultivation of the individual into the 'Superior Person'. For Confucius, the Superior Person is someone who manages to combine selflessness and understanding in private life and courteousness in public life. Confucius's pronouncements on the cultivation of the gentleman in *The Analects*, provide a major insight into his ideal of the Superior Person. In this work, he develops a number of maxims which he regarded as essential to the proper conduct of the gentleman:

The Master said:

'*The gentleman is at ease without being arrogant; the small man is arrogant without being at ease.*'

Tzu-lu asked:

'*What must a man be like before he deserves to be called a Gentleman?*'

The Master said:

'*One who is, on the one hand, earnest and keen and, on the other, genial, deserves to be called a Gentleman – earnest and keen amongst friends and genial amongst brothers.*'

The values evident in these maxims should be continually present in what Confucius called the 'Five Constant Relationships', which are:

1. Parent and child
2. Husband and wife
3. Elder sibling and junior sibling
4. Elder friend and junior friend
5. Ruler and subject.

The following passage sums up the unity of Confucius's teachings:

'*If there is righteousness in the heart, there will be beauty in the character. If there is beauty in the character, there will be harmony in the home. If there be harmony in the home, there will be order in the nation. If there be order in the nation, there will be peace in the world.*'

CONFUCIANISM

The moral, philosophical and political teachings of Confucianism represent one of the most remarkable phenomena of human thought. Its impressive qualities lie in the fact that its influence, which has been religious in nature, has not been led by any divine status. Confucius was strictly a teacher and philosopher, not a divine prophet, and the sheer scale of his influence is therefore unparalleled. Until the Communist Revolution, every Chinese child would learn, by heart, the main principles of Confucius's teachings, and a superior knowledge of them was assessed prior to acceptance in many areas of public life.

CONFUCIANISM DOMINATED LIFE IN CHINA UNTIL THE REVOLUTION IN 1949. THE REPUBLIC REPLACED THE TEACHINGS OF CONFUCIUS WITH THEIR OWN DOCTRINE. LEFT: YOUNG CHINESE DEMONSTRATE THEIR SUPPORT FOR MAO'S CULTURAL REVOLUTION BY WAVING COPIES OF HIS FAMOUS *LITTLE RED BOOK*.

THE CHRISTIAN PHILOSOPHERS

As Christianity dominated Europe, scholars sought to combine philosophy with theology and adapt the ideas of the Ancient Greeks to reflect Christian beliefs. Their work, far from being fettered by Christian ideology, was vital in the advancement of philosophical investigations

CHAPTER THREE

THE BIRTH OF CHRISTIAN EUROPE

To understand Christian Europe, we must understand the uniqueness of European culture and its thinking. Western thinking, which grew through both stories and philosophies, concerned itself with explaining the distinctiveness of the Western mind. In doing so, it helped develop a notion of Europe which was central to the evolution of Christian philosophy. The Romans first conceived the idea of Europe in the 2nd century. They used it to denote the difference between western Roman troops – 'European' – and eastern troops – 'the Orientals'. However, it was through the philosophy and theology of Christianity that Europe truly defined itself.

DAWN OF CHRISTIANITY

The moral, philosophical and religious beliefs of the early Christians in the Roman empire were neither new nor unique. The New Testament had much in common with Pagan and Greek religion, for example the idea that all men are equal before God. In order to be accepted, Christianity had to draw upon established religious culture. However, the key to establishing religious obedience to Christianity was St Paul's statement in the New Testament: 'Let every soul be subject unto the higher powers. For there is no power but that of God: the powers that be are ordained of God. Whosoever therefore resisteth the power, resisteth the ordinance of God; and they that resisteth shall receive to themselves damnation.'

The key period in the establishment of Christianity, and the Catholic Church, in Europe was the 4th century. During the 1st century, the so-called Doctors of the Western Church, St Ambrose, St Jerome and St Augustine, unified and rationalized Christian doctrine. It was through the teachings of Ambrose that the Church justified its sphere of autonomy; through Jerome, the Bible was translated and edited; and through Augustine, Catholicism was given philosophical justification. It was also during this period that a succession of European emperors adopted Catholicism as an official religion.

EAST VERSUS WEST?

The conflict between Islam and the emerging world of Christianity is central to the turbulent history of Christianity and Europe. Western philosophy and theology has long depicted the social and political institutions of the East as tyrannical. The result of this was that a powerful myth emerged suggesting that European Christianity was born out of the need to unify against the oppressive and barbaric social practices of the East. Ironically, many of the ideas and institutions of Christian Europe undoubtedly came from the East and during conflicts between European emperors and Eastern empires, the Islamic world was often a lot more civilised than Europe.

RICHARD I AND SALADIN AT ASCALON. ALTHOUGH SALADIN RECAPTURED JERUSALEM FROM THE CHRISTIANS, THEY ADMIRED HIM FOR HIS GENEROUS TREATMENT OF PRISONERS AND HIS ENCOURAGEMENT OF EAST–WEST TRADE.

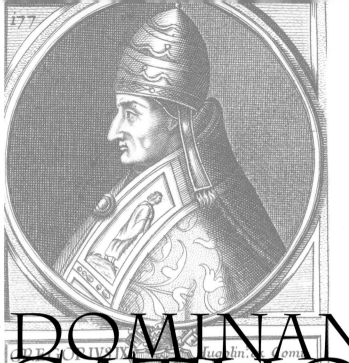

DOMINANCE OF CATHOLICISM

The Roman Catholic Church drew its model for governance from the Roman empire in order to create a durable and powerful structure. Control of cultural activities, education, theology, public festivals and, of course, religious ceremonies resided in the Church of Rome. Catholicism dominated the culture of the most civilised centres of European civilisation, so the literature and philosophy during the Dark to Middle Ages rarely ventured outside the accepted theological doctrines of St Augustine (written in the 4th and 5th centuries). The treasures of Classical literature from Ancient Greece and Rome were barely kept alive and those that were read were re-interpreted to suit the Christian faith. Until the 11th century, Europe's scholarly community was tiny.

However, whilst the Church developed more control over European culture, its influence on kings and emperors was limited and it was often called upon to justify the barbarism of European rulers. Kings would use bishops, and even the Pope, for their own political ends. These political struggles often resulted in a lot of clergymen being kidnapped and killed. In most cases, the clergy outside Rome operated under the financial and political jurisdiction of kings.

POPE GREGORY VII

By the 11th century the Church was in need of reform and re-invention. This it received through the papacy of Pope Gregory VII. First he strengthened and purified the clergy. Through the doctrine of transubstantiation only the priest could perform the ritual of Mass and could also determine whether a person would go to heaven or hell. Before this reform, the sinner could repent his sins and confirm his faith on his deathbed, which meant the Church had only limited control over his activities during life. Gregory's reforms also enabled priests to excommunicate heretics. This meant that, if the heretic were not accepted back into the Church before his death, he would go to hell.

Gregory also introduced celibacy into the priesthood. This reform benefited the Church of Rome in two ways. Firstly, priests and bishops who had married and had children were able to pass their title and lands on to their sons, thus taking away vital control of appointment from Rome. Secondly, celibacy distanced priests from ordinary people and ensured clergy received greater respect.

Other reforms concerned the relationship between the Pope and Europe's kings. In 1075 the *Dictatus Papae* declared, 'The Pope is the

one representative of God on earth; he bears the keys of heaven and hell.' A king's authority to rule was bestowed upon him by the Pope. The Pope was the king of kings. Gregory's reforms had led to a series of political struggles and eventually the German state went outside Rome's authority. Nonetheless, the reforms Gregory instituted became the foundation of Catholic supremacy in Europe for the next six centuries.

THE INQUISITION

The event which most powerfully illustrates the Church's supremacy was the Inquisition. Founded by Pope Gregory IX in 1233, the Inquisition emerged in response to the growing popularity of heretic creeds. Had the Inquisition not been established, the result would have been a revolt against the Church of similar proportions to that which followed in the 16th century.

The aim of the Inquisition was to seek out heresy rather than wait for it to manifest itself. Courts were set up to judge the guilt of potential heretics. At first these courts were manned by bishops, but later the task fell to the Dominican and Franciscan friars. Those accused of heresy were ordered to appear before the Inquisition and their chances of survival were very slim. If they failed to confess to heresy, they would be horribly tortured and if a confession was still not forthcoming, they would be burned at the

stake. If the accused confessed to heresy, they would be saved the horror of the stake and fined instead. But if they could not pay the fine, they would be thrown into prison where they would, in all probability, endure a slow and painful death.

The most ruthless branches of the Inquisition were in France and Spain where the accused had no right to counsel. In these regions, if the state did not carry out appropriate punishment, those responsible for punishment were subjected to the Inquisition's wrath. The Dominican and Franciscan orders at the heart of the Inquisition also produced the great scholastic and philosophical works of the 13th and 14th century – this fact should not be ignored when considering the apparently revolutionary philosophies.

INQUISITION REVISITED

The Inquisition of the 13th and 14th centuries helped to strengthen the Church's authority. In the 16th century the Church was once again under threat and, so, the Inquisition was revived. But on this occasion it merely strengthened the dissenting voices of Puritanism and Protestantism and it failed to quash the emerging popularity of scientific reason.

St Augustine's contribution to human thought came during a period of great social and political change in Europe. The Roman empire had fallen and in its wake Europe lapsed into the Dark Ages. This era was characterised by religious fanaticism, superstition and barbarous cruelty. The Dark Ages also saw the birth of the organised religions of European Christianity and the work of St Augustine was a major force in this development. Augustine's theology was a fundamental source of doctrine for Christian religion over the next thousand years. It gave Christianity a coherent belief system which the Old Testament on its own could not have provided.

ST AUGUSTINE
(354–430)

THEOLOGY OR PHILOSOPHY?

Augustine's writings are on the borders of philosophy and theology. His work was dedicated to reconciling speculative, critical thought with scripture. In Augustine, therefore, philosophy is dissolved into theology. However, this dissolution is never complete because whilst he seeks further justification of God and God's creations, his work is not a simple statement of religious doctrine. It is, irreducibly, a philosophical justification of Christianity and takes the form of a modification of Platonic ideas to serve the scripture.

DEVIL HOLDING THE BOOK OF VICES IN FRONT OF ST AUGUSTINE – ST AUGUSTINE BELIEVED THAT AS PUNISHMENT FOR ADAM'S SIN THE WORLD WAS DIVIDED INTO MORAL AND IMMORAL BEINGS.

GOD AND THE ACT OF CREATION

Plato's central argument was that the world was made up of eternal substances given by the gods. Those substances, such as virtue, can only be known in their purest form by God, who therefore had absolute knowledge. This knowledge could, nonetheless, be tapped into, but not completely consumed, by the philosopher. In an effort to recognise Plato's wisdom and justify the Old Testament, Augustine modified Plato's doctrine in *Confessions* (397–400) and *De Libero Arbitrio* (391–395). Augustine believed that God has absolute knowledge as the original source of all experience and nature. He also adopted Plato's assertion that God created the eternal substances from which human existence is derived. He went on to state that God created the world from nothing and before God created the world nothing existed, because before creation time cannot exist. Augustine gave God's authority an absolute foundation which was lacking in Plato's work.

ORIGINAL SIN

In *On the Trinity* (399-412), Augustine argued that God arbitrarily divided the world into moral and immoral beings. This act of damnation on humankind was carried out to punish Adam's sin in succumbing to temptation. Those tempted by evil were condemned by God. This condemnation is the burden of all humankind. To save one's soul from eternal damnation one must overcome the temptation of evil. The source of evil is the lust of the human senses which is independent of the will of the human soul – the human incarnation of God's will. To be virtuous, therefore, is to control the body's will. However, Augustine somewhat paradoxically explains that it is God's will which determines that some and

not others succumb to the temptation of evil. Curiously, this means that one can be condemned to eternal damnation by God unless one has control of one's will, but failure to control one's will is antecedently prescribed by God. The ferocity of the doctrine of original sin, as theorised by Augustine, became the source of some harsh religious practices in Christian Europe.

CHURCH AND STATE

During Augustine's time, neither the Church nor the State had taken on their modern form. The Church had little in common with the mass organised religion of Roman Catholicism in the 11th–12th centuries, and the state had not yet emerged as an all-powerful authority. Nonetheless, Augustine's theory on the relationship between religious and political spheres was used to justify the practices of both in the Middle and Medieval Ages. For Augustine the state, though separate, should abide by the practices and teachings of the Church. This belief was used as a justification of absolutism in Europe – to rule in accordance with religious practice, it was argued, must necessarily be to rule absolutely. Through this mutual justification, the Church and state grew in strength.

Little is known about Scot's early years in Ireland, though it is clear that, at the time, Ireland was one of the few centres of Classical learning. It was largely cut off from Rome and, whilst Christian, obedience to Catholic doctrine was weak. In the 840s Scot was invited to France by Charles the Bald to arbitrate in a theological dispute. His first known venture in philosophy and theology was a product of this arbitration, a treatise entitled *On Divine Predestination*. In the treatise, Scot questioned the work of St Augustine which had been the foundation of Catholic teaching for 500 years. In most cases, questioning Augustine's authority would have been punished by excommunication or death, but under the patronage of Charles the Bald, Scot managed to avoid such consequences. However, the circumstances of his eventual death are unknown.

JOHN DU SCOT (800–77)

Towards the end of the 9th and 10th centuries a new breed of scholar emerged in Europe. Before this time scholars were rare. The first of this new breed was Irishman John du Scot. Scot, unlike his predecessors, was prepared to indulge in Classical scholarship and not merely for the benefit of the Church. A great deal of Classical literature was preserved but little was studied and Scot's training as a Classical Greek scholar was the foundation for what was considered his near-heretical rationality.

ABOVE: JOHN DU SCOT'S FIRST DOCUMENTED WORK OF PHILOSOPHY, *ON DIVINE PREDESTINATION*, WAS INSPIRED BY AN INVITATION FROM CHARLES THE BALD OF FRANCE TO ARBITRATE IN A THEOLOGICAL DISPUTE.

REASON VERSUS RELIGION

Scot challenged Augustine's view of the relationship between God's will and the free will of men. Augustine had argued that man's will is pre-ordained by God, which means that the chances of leading a virtuous life on earth are predetermined by God. Scot disagreed and asserted that men do have free will because the will of God is the free will of men's pursuit of reason. For Scot reason presides over religion; reason is God's truth and religion is merely the worship of God. Therefore one should not confuse reason with religious doctrine. God's will is above religious doctrine.

THE DIVISION OF NATURE

However, Scot was by no means a complete secularist; despite appearances to the contrary he had no intention of questioning the

absolute authority of God. This is made clear in Scot's most significant work, which was called *On the Division of Nature*. It was here that Scot also brought his Classical Greek scholarship to bear upon theology. In the book he contends that Nature is divided into four classes: (1) What creates and is not created. Quite simply this is God. (2) What creates and is created. In answer to this Scot borrows Plato's ideas, i.e. that the world is made up of universal substances out of which everything particular is created. Once the process of creation gets to this stage God's will is present but more distant in that humanity creates its own particularities out of the universals that have been created by God. (3) What is created but does not create, i.e. the invisible objects of space and time. (4) What neither creates nor is created. The answer to this once again is God. This may seem to contradict the first point, indeed logically it does and the contradiction is intentional. It is meant to signify his belief that in order to create, God must be a 'thing'

which creates, therefore God cannot 'create' as such because by definition a thing must have been created and God cannot have been created if he is the supreme being. The fact that Scot thought that God neither creates nor is created was equal to the worst kind of heresy in the 9th century in that it could be interpreted as demeaning the supreme being.

To the modern reader, not well versed in Catholic doctrine, the differences between John du Scot and his contemporaries may appear to be minor, but at the time this was not the case. Though Scot escaped punishment his work was widely condemned as heretical. This was largely because Scot regarded rationality rather than theology as the foundation of existence.

'For Scot the will of God is the free will of men's pursuit of reason. Reason presides over religion; reason is God's truth and religion is merely worship.'

THOMAS AQUINAS (1225–74)

The work of Thomas Aquinas is the chief source of modern Catholic theology. His writing was part of a cultural revolution in Europe in the 13th century. Universities were established all over Europe and the teaching of the 'seven liberal arts' (grammar, logic, rhetoric, arithmetic, geometry, music and astronomy) was received by increasing numbers of students. This expansion of the scholarly world helped create an atmosphere in which the received doctrines of the Catholic Church, founded upon the theology of Augustine, were challenged. Aquinas challenged dominant Catholic theology by embracing writings derived from the re-appraisal of ancient scholarship.

FAMILY DISAPPROVAL

Aquinas was born in Naples in 1225 and at the age of five was sent to the Benedictine abbey of Monte Cassino. He later studied at the newly established University of Naples but at 21 he was sent to prison at his family's request for choosing to become a Dominican friar. In the 13th century a friar was a lowly figure who often had to beg for subsistence, and this greatly offended the aristocratic sensibilities of the Aquinas family.

Whilst imprisoned Aquinas wrote his first treatise on theology and philosophy, focusing upon logic. When he was 30 Aquinas accepted the chair in theology at the University of Paris. During his time in Paris, Aquinas was subject to the influence of Dominican scholars who studied Aristotle. In the early 13th century, Plato was still the dominant Classical figure and the work of Aristotle was often regarded as heretical. After only three years in Paris, Aquinas returned to Italy where he wrote his most important work, *Summa contra Gentiles*, in 1264. Aquinas remained an energetic teacher and theologian throughout the rest of his life, and he set up various schools and assemblies in Florence, Paris and Naples. His work was eventually condemned by the universities of Paris and Oxford and it was not until 50 years after his death that it received the appreciation it deserved.

GOD AND NATURE

The notion that the existence of God needed to be justified was a flirtation with heresy. For to seek to prove the existence of God was to beg the question that God might not exist. If the existence of God need not be proven then nor did his teachings or creations. For a long time Catholic theology merely restated received doctrine and justified (using the established theological framework provided by Augustine) new moral codes needed for particular circumstances.

Thomas Aquinas helped to bring Catholic philosophy out of this impasse by arguing that improving our understanding of the natural world did not threaten the Catholic faith. He argued that a greater understanding of the laws of nature would deepen our respect for God's creations. If God's most glorious creation was man then developing man's reason was a way of celebrating God's glory.

Aquinas' chief contribution, in terms of philosophy, was to loosen Plato's grip on scholastic thinking. Through Augustine in the 4th century, Plato's notion of a world of transcendent ideas was re-interpreted as divinely ordained. According to both Plato and Augustine, all human knowledge was derived from *universals* (ideas). For Thomas Aquinas the reverse is true. All human knowledge is derived from *particulars* which can be abstracted into universal ideas. It appears, on the surface, that Aquinas is questioning the absoluteness of God's knowledge by, apparently, taking away a supposed element of God's creation (i.e. the universal ideas from which the forms that make up the world are created). However, this is not the case. Aquinas believed that God's creation of the world was continuous; God creates everything including human beings.

"In reply to the question 'is there such a thing as fate?' we might give the name fate to the order impressed by providence but it is wiser not to do so as fate is a pagan word."

ROGER BACON

Roger Bacon's rebelliousness captured the spirit of the Franciscan order, though he often courted controversy with his fellow Franciscans. He was most famous for using scientific experiment as a way of uncovering natural law. In the 13th century any form of experimental science performed by a member of the Catholic Church was considered to be heretical. By also indulging in alchemy and magic Bacon tempted the wrath of the Church even further. In 1278 he was sent to prison for 14 years.

THE FRANCISCANS

The Franciscans, alongside the Dominicans, were at the centre of the religious and scholarly enlightenment of the 13th and 14th centuries. The scholars of the Franciscan order were among the first to challenge radically the scholastic orthodoxy which had been established a thousand years earlier by Augustine. They also played a large part in the development of new universities in the 14th century. Their sustained challenge to scholastic orthodoxy saw the Franciscans become a populist movement; this status was enhanced by a willingness to address issues of poverty. The three most important Franciscans were Roger Bacon, Dunus Scotus and William of Occam.

DUNUS SCOTUS

Along with attempts to revise the theological doctrines of St Augustine, the most important philosophical and theological debate of the 13th century was that between Thomas Aquinas (a Dominican) and the Franciscans. The work of Dunus Scotus was very central to this debate. The focus of the debate was the theological re-interpretation of Plato and Aristotle. The Franciscans were on the side of Plato. The key issue in this debate was the Ancient Greek question of essence, i.e. does each thing contain an individual essence, or are all things within a particular form made of the same essence. Scotus claimed that every identifiable thing has its own particular essence? This theme is still the cause of great controversy in modern philosophy – is the world made up of universal forms, essences and laws or just particular things?

WILLIAM OF OCCAM

William of Occam, born in 1285 in the English village of Occam, became the most significant Franciscan scholar. His theology was so controversial that he was forced to seek the protection of the Emperor of Bavaria, famously declaring, 'defend me with the sword,

"Nothing can be known naturally in itself unless it is known intuitively" – William of Occam

and I will defend you with the pen.' Occam's controversy surrounded his pseudo-scientific beliefs and some contemporary thinkers have argued that the origins of the modern scientific view can be found in Occam's work. However, this is probably stretching his influence more than is credible. In fact, Occam's philosophy was as much about purifying established philosophy as it was about pushing philosophy forward.

OCCAM'S RAZOR

The aspect of Occam's work most responsible for interpretations of him as 'a modern' is captured in his famous maxim: 'It is vain to do with more what can be done with fewer'. This maxim, which is often called Occam's razor, is based on Occam's philosophy of logic. He argued that there existed no universal forms outside of the human mind, therefore universal concepts, which name particular things outside the mind, are a subject for logic and grammar rather than metaphysics. For Occam, words and concepts are not real, only 'particular things-in-themselves' are real. However, particular things do not necessarily correspond to their concepts, names or words.

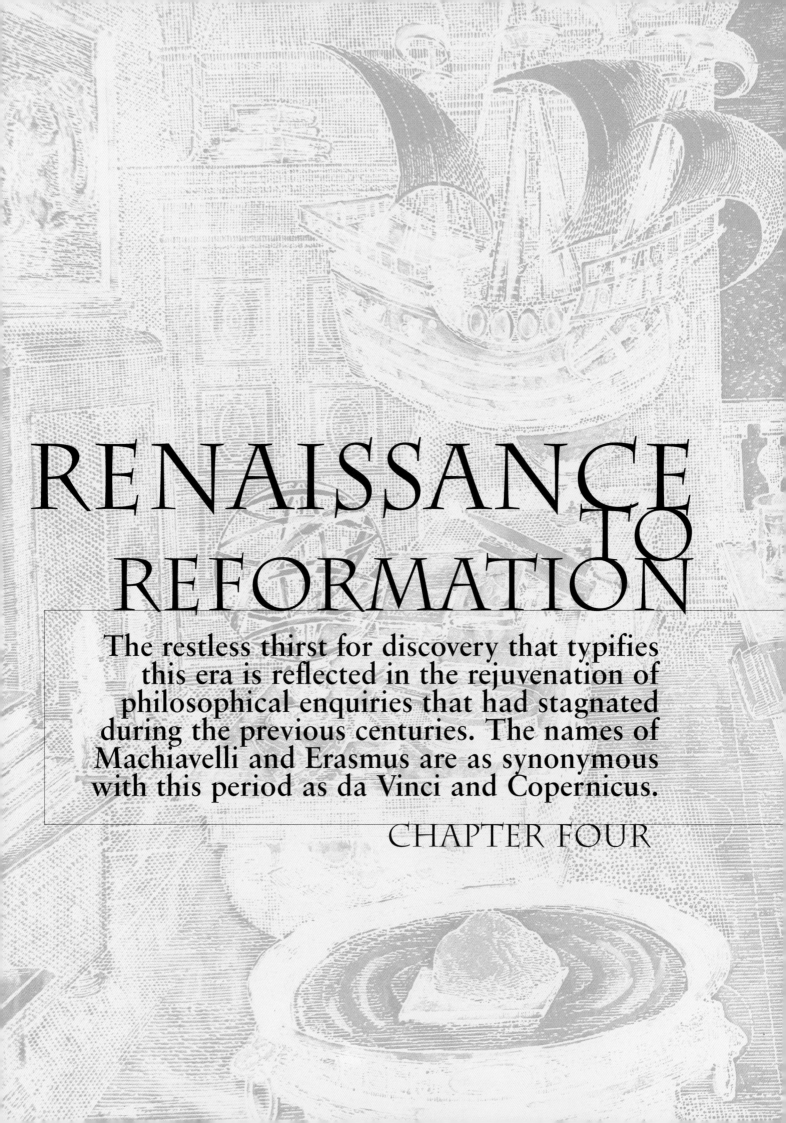

RENAISSANCE TO REFORMATION

The restless thirst for discovery that typifies
this era is reflected in the rejuvenation of
philosophical enquiries that had stagnated
during the previous centuries. The names of
Machiavelli and Erasmus are as synonymous
with this period as da Vinci and Copernicus.

CHAPTER FOUR

THE RENAISSANCE

The incessant intellectual energy which characterises the contemporary world was born in the Renaissance. In the 14th and 15th centuries, Europe woke from a thousand years of cultural stagnation by rediscovering the cultural riches of antiquity. Italy spearheaded this awakening by cultivating the study of ancient Greece and Rome. This surpassed the use the scholastics and the Catholic Church had previously made of older knowledge. The new spirit of curiosity about the ancient world became the foundation upon which the scientific discoveries and literary and artistic creativity of the Renaissance flourished. Philosophical speculation thrived in this atmosphere.

ITALY AND THE RENAISSANCE

The spirit of the Renaissance was evident throughout northern Europe, but its spiritual home was undoubtedly Italy. To be more accur-ate, since Italy did not exist in this period as a nation state, the Renaissance flourished among the city states which now constitute Italy. In terms of intellectual endeavour, and indeed political prominence, the most important city states were Florence and Venice. Florence was the home of Petrarch, Italy's poetic father. Petrarch's poetry is said to mark the dawn of Italy's intellectual renaissance. The spiritual disciples of Petrarch

HUMANISTS, LIKE ITALIAN SCHOLAR GIOVANNI (LEFT), SOUGHT TO RETURN THE TEXTS OF ANTIQUITY TO THEIR ORIGINAL STATE – FREE FROM INTERPRETATION.

scoured Europe for old manuscripts which they used to build up new libraries and seats of learning. Education and learning became so fashionable that scholars became public figures, some even celebrated heroes. This was especially the case after the Medici family had overthrown the old Florentine nobility to create a new environment in which scholarly and artistic endeavour could flourish.

THE DISCOVERY OF THE WORLD

The intellectual energy of the Renaissance also sparked an adventurous, exploratory spirit in Europe. The scientific discoveries of the Renaissance, most notably the astrological ones, were combined with the further exploration of the corners of the globe. In 1492 Columbus discovered America for the Europeans and the Portuguese rounded the Cape for the first time in 1497. This was

> ### 'Copernicus's great scientific discoveries disturbed the received view of the universe, with God at the summit, earth at the base and men and angels in between.'

followed in 1507 by Copernicus's great scientific discovery: a revolutionary new view of the solar system. Copernicus claimed to have discovered that the sun rather than the earth was the centre of the universe. This upset the received view of the universe as held captive by the chain of being – God at the summit, earth at the base and men and angels in between.

THE DISCOVERY OF MAN

The Renaissance is undoubtedly most famous for its art, and, in particular, the work of Michelangelo. However, Renaissance art had a much wider significance than its decorative splendour. The new art was founded upon a desire among artists to reflect a deepening knowledge of man by using more accurate representations in painting and sculpture. The objective of the artist became to combine respect for sacred legend, with concern for beauty and for more accurate depiction.

THE HUMANISTS

The discovery of the world through scientific and geographic exploration and the study of man in the new forms of painting formed the background of the philosophical activity of the period. The movement that is most commonly associated with the Renaissance is Humanism, although the term Humanism only became common terminology in the 19th century. The Humanist movement was not one with specific ideologies – rather it was dedicated to the study of the cultural artefacts of human beings as opposed to the divine creations of God. Humanists did this by renewing interest in the literary classics of antiquity. Their concern to rewrite texts of antiquity free from the very subjective translations that had been written through centuries of interpretation, gave them a deeper sense of how culture is shaped by institutions, customs and ideas.

The Reformation and the resultant structural changes to Europe's religious make-up had a profound effect on the development of Western thought. The religious, political and philosophical doctrines of the Reformation period are, therefore, important indicators of Europe's cultural development. The structural changes began with a widespread questioning of the Roman Catholic Church and the status of the Pope. In the late 15th century a resentment of the corruption, indulgences and moral and political power of the Catholic Church had developed. The most symbolic expression of this resentment came when Martin Luther nailed his 95 theses against indulgence to the gates of the castle church at Wittenberg in 1517. This was the beginning of Protestantism and Puritanism as an intellectual movement in northern Europe.

The fragmentation of Christian doctrine and practice created religious tension and led many people to question how societies should be governed. European states now had to cope with religious diversity within their borders. The reaction of monarchy and statesmen was, in many cases, to strengthen absolutism either in support or opposition to the papacy. The reaction in terms of philosophical discourse was increased speculation on the question of political power and its relationship to human nature. This debate was carried out separately from theology. The work of Machiavelli and later Hobbes provide the most striking examples of the new philosophical discourse.

THE REFORMATION

MARTIN LUTHER

Luther was born in 1483 at Eisleben, central Germany, the spiritual home of the Reformation. He was a professor of biblical theology at Wittenburg and his theological writing changed the course of European history. His aim was to rediscover the original Gospel; as it had been before it was deformed by medieval theology. He thought that there was a gulf between the word of God represented in scripture and the Church as an institution. Luther argued that there is nothing in scripture which justifies papal power and its elaborate rituals. For Luther, true faith in God is best expressed in the activities of daily life rather than pilgrimages or sacred rituals. One can serve God by serving one's neighbour rather than the Church. After some delay, Rome eventually excommunicated Luther, sparking a religious conflict which lasted throughout the 16th century.

CALVIN

John Calvin (1509–64) occupied the same religious and intellectual territory as Luther. However, unlike Luther, Calvin encouraged whole states to reject the Catholic Church. He was able to put this rejection into practice when he became head of the Church in Geneva in 1541. Calvin preached a stricter obedience to moral conduct than the Catholic Church, which placed more emphasis on religious obedience through ritual. In Calvin's Geneva, all areas of private and public life

THE FOCUS OF MUCH OF THE ANTI-CATHOLIC SENTIMENT THAT SPREAD ACROSS EUROPE WAS THE PAPACY, WHICH WAS WIDELY SEEN BY THOSE WHO OPPOSED THE CATHOLIC CHURCH AS THOROUGHLY CORRUPT AND ILLEGITIMATE.

were scrutinised. In some ways, it was simply a different kind of absolutism and not unlike Catholicism practised by European monarchies. The practice of Calvinism was notable for its repression.

Machiavelli's writings have been invested with a legendary quality, although at the time they were regarded as the work of the devil. Principally, Machiavelli was a political philosopher and he was the first philosopher to study the mechanics of political power as a subject beyond, if not exclusive of, moral doctrine. His work is surrounded by myth and infamy, and it is widely misunderstood.

NICCOLÒ MACHIAVELLI (1469–1527)

THE DIPLOMAT

In 1494 Florence, the city where Machiavelli lived, fell under the reign of the French and Spanish respectively. Its fall came after a period of relative stability and cultural advancement, helped by a diplomatic alliance of the five most powerful Italian city states: Venice, Milan, Naples, the Papacy and Florence itself (which was ruled by Lorenzo de' Medici). The manner in which his beloved Florence was forced to relinquish its power made a powerful impression on Machiavelli. This political interest culminated in Machiavelli's appointment as secretary and Second Chancellor in the Florentine government. The post mainly involved diplomatic duties, which brought Machiavelli closer to the manipulative and vengeful world of European politics. In 1512 after the return of the Medici to power in

Florence, Machiavelli was dismissed from his post and subsequently embarked on his career as a 'man of letters'. His first, and most famous, book *The Prince* (1513) drew upon his experiences as a diplomat and was written in the form of advice on the art of governing to Lorenzo II of Florence. In the accompanying letter he writes: 'Now, I am anxious to offer myself to Your Magnificence with some token of my devotion to you, and I have not found among my belongings anything as dear to me or that I value as much as my understanding of the deeds of great men . . .'

THE PRINCE

In *The Prince*, Machiavelli claims he is writing a new kind of political theory. His bold claim was based on his concern to draw upon the experience of history rather than any moral or abstract principles. He wanted to persuade his contemporaries that the practice of governing could only be judged in relation to the end to which its practitioners strived. The first principle of governing is the consolidation of power and so the success of rulers can only be

assessed by their political strength. This does not mean that the end justifies the means, because Machiavelli believed that when the means of ruling is distracted from the need to consolidate power the security of power is threatened.

For Machiavelli a virtuous Prince is not one who rules by the laws of good and evil but one who retains 'a willingness to do whatever may be necessary for the pursuit of civic glory'. The term Machiavellian is often used to describe a power-hungry tyrant, but this is a misuse of Machiavelli's advice. Machiavelli is not suggesting that rulers should rule tyranni- cally – very often those that do so ignore Machiavelli's advice. For Machiavelli advised that the Prince 'should determine to avoid anything which will make him hated and despised'. This means that while he must be above morality he ignores it at his peril.

THE DISCOURSES

The impression of Machiavelli's thought gained by reading *The Prince* is of a political philosopher unconcerned with the forms of government, other than their effect on the Prince's power. But this is a distorted picture of Machiavelli. In *The Discourses* Machiavelli

OPPOSITE PAGE: BUST OF MACHIAVELLI WHO THOUGHT HE WAS RESPONSIBLE FOR A NEW TYPE OF POLITICAL THEORY.
TOP: *THE PRINCE* WAS DEDICATED TO LORENZO DE MEDICI.
ABOVE: *MURDER OF CAESAR* BY KARL T. VON PILOTY – MACHIAVELLI THOUGHT A SECURE RULER WOULD ALWAYS CONSOLIDATE POWER.

reflects more soberly on the end to which his own advice should be directed. From this work, it is clear he is a republican and an early modern liberal who writes belovedly about liberty and constitution.

ERASMUS (1466–1536)

The Renaissance is popularly regarded as a brilliant and colourful period of Italian history which gave the world Leonardo da Vinci, Michelangelo and Machiavelli. However, though not as colourful, there was a renaissance in northern Europe. The Northern Renaissance was much less questioning of religious authority and much more concerned with slow gradual reform and adaptation of ecclesiastical practice. Erasmus, who was born in Rotterdam, Holland, was a key figure in the Northern Renaissance. Unlike his more vigorously reformist successors, he was concerned with advancing the quality of learning and education given by the Catholic Church. He was certainly not an advocate of the Reformation. However, in his concern for the values of accuracy, and grammatical and rhetorical elegance, Erasmus's early modern temperament was evident. This temperament was anti-intellectual; Erasmus valued simplicity above intellectual complexity, and the influence of his work was based on its moral force rather than its philosophical originality.

IN PRAISE OF FOLLY

The only book by Erasmus which is still widely available is *The Praise of Folly*. Erasmus argued that striving for happiness as the object of life is folly. This is because in order to be happy we must delude ourselves through exaggerated conceit, self-love and flattery. Even happiness in friendship is based on folly: 'winking at your friend's faults, passing over them, turning a blind eye, building up illusions, treating obvious faults as virtues – isn't all that related to folly'. However, if one attempted to live life by wisdom alone, one would never consider, for example, the virtues of the married life: 'What man would be willing to offer his neck to the altar of matrimony if he applied the usual practice of the wise man and first weighed up its disadvantages as a way of life? Or what woman would ever agree to take a husband if she knew or

TOP: FOR ERASMUS SIMPLICITY AND ELEGANCE OF STYLE IN PHILOSOPHY WERE VIRTUES MORE WORTHY THAN COMPLEXITY WHICH MOST PHILOSOPHERS EXERCISED. ABOVE: IN HIS BOOK, *IN PRAISE OF FOLLY*, ERASMUS EXPLAINS HOW THE OBJECTS OF OUR HAPPINESS ARE A DELUSION.

thought about the pains and dangers of child-birth and the trouble of bringing up children? So if you owe your existence to wedlock, you owe the fact of wedlock to madness . . .'

For Erasmus the wisest man is furthest from happiness. Erasmus pokes fun at the philosopher who 'has combed through his bookcases in order to master the whole of divinity' and 'nibbles at a dry bean and carries on a non-stop war with bugs and lice' in order to pursue his scholarly ambitions. Those scholarly ambitions are in any case flawed because one cannot hope to master the totality of any subject.

According to Erasmus, the best form of enlightenment can be found in the foundations of education, namely rhetorical elegance, grammatical correctness and style. Bare facts and complicated formulae have a temporary existence in the memory and the teaching of

ABOVE: *THE BATTLE OF FLODDEN* (1513) – ERASMUS DENOUNCED THE VIOLENT ENFORCEMENT OF THEOLOGY AND WROTE: 'THEIR [POPES'] ONLY WEAPONS OUGHT TO BE THOSE OF THE SPIRIT.'

LEFT: ERASMUS'S COMMENTARY ON WHAT HE SAW AS THE ILLUSIONS OF MODERN LIFE CAN BE COMPARED TO THE WRITINGS OF FELLOW NORTHERN RENAISSANCE THINKERS LIKE THOMAS MORE WHO WROTE *UTOPIA* AND WHOM ERASMUS MET WHILST IN LONDON.

them should be secondary. The best education can be found in reading the classics whereby one can note particular examples of rhetorical elegance, argumentative style and eloquent but pithy maxims.

This concern for education may not appear particularly philosophical. However, when Erasmus was writing the subject of self-cultivation was hotly contested and involved a range of moral and political issues. Erasmus's legacy is that his anti-intellectualism and promotion of elegance and eloquence above scientific and factual learning remains the foundation of education in most Western public schools.

"Woe unto you, scribes and pharisees, . . . I left you but one precedent, of loving another, which I do not hear any plead that he has faithfully discharged."

The name of Michel de Montaigne is often absent from lists of the great philosophers. This is, in part, because even a sympathetic account of his work cannot suggest that his influence is equal to that of Hobbes or Erasmus. But it is also because his work was unsystematic and was in essay form rather than treatise. However, there was purpose behind Montaigne's unsystematic approach to philosophy. He epitomised certain tendencies in the philosophy of the Renaissance–Reformation period. Montaigne's formative years coincided with a period of religious upheaval in Europe and the Reformation undoubtedly sharpened Montaigne's awareness of the diversity of religious belief. As a member of the French nobility, he was also taught to look down on obsession with systematic study – the principal knowledge of the nobleman being his cultivation as a gentleman. Montaigne's essays have an autobiographical tone which reflects this. Aside from his philosophical inclinations, Montaigne served as Mayor in Bordeaux, and later acted as an adviser to leaders of the Reformation and the counter-Reformation.

MONTAIGNE
(1533–92)

THE SCEPTIC

In his most important work, *The Essays*, Montaigne appeals to the sceptical philosophy of late Greek antiquity, which he brought to bear on the issues of his age. On the beams of his study room Montaigne had inscribed 'all that is certain is that nothing is certain' and 'I

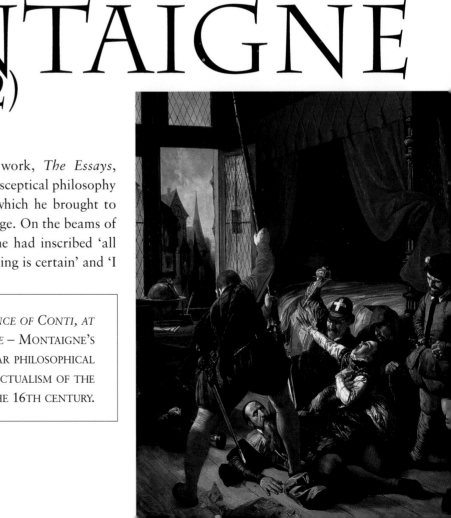

The Assassination of Briou, tutor to the Prince of Conti, at the St Bartholomew's Day Massacre – Montaigne's aristocratic background fuelled his particular philosophical scepticism, drawn from the anti-intellectualism of the French aristocracy in the 16th century.

suspend judgement'. Faced with a world where cultural plurality harnessed different values and perceptions, there must be no alternative to scepticism about the certainty of human knowledge. This variety of experience forced Montaigne to suspend judgement. In the case of moral values, this approach is particularly valuable; Montaigne gives examples of African cultures whose values are alien to Europeans but unquestioned in their own society. Even within our culture the slightest difference in our state of being can affect the views we have of the world. For Montaigne, human knowledge is far too unreliable; it is coloured

by too many different factors to be assessed with certainty. As he remarks, 'No two men ever had the same opinion of the same thing'. Like Socrates who said he knew only that he knew nothing, Montaigne equates dogmatism with ignorance and the unsystematic style of his philosophy reflects his belief that we give order to human knowledge in vain.

For most contemporary philosophers Montaigne's scepticism would be far too crude to accept. However, his views certainly have a contemporary feel to them. One must be careful in equating Montaigne's acceptance of cultural diversity as liberal; his scepticism was very much an aristocratic, philosophical scepticism drawn from the Ancient Greeks.

THE POLITICS

Despite his scepticism Montaigne promoted conformity to dominant traditions. He employed his scepticism in a politically conservative manner and argued, 'in public affairs, there is no course so bad, provided that it is stable and traditional, that is not better than change and alteration...It is easy enough to criticize a political system...But to establish a better regime in place of the one which has been destroyed, there is the problem.' Montaigne thought that the terror and disruption brought by radical change was a high price to pay for imposing new values about which we cannot be certain and which often derive from an enforced ignorance of reality.

Bacon, like most philosophers, was driven by the emerging spirit of his age. That spirit was concerned with scientific exploration. Bacon's contribution to philosophy was to promote that spirit and loosen the grip of Aristotle's philosophy of logic which had held science, philosophy and theology captive for centuries.

For much of his life, however, Bacon was concerned with political matters. His father had been involved with state affairs and Bacon's career in politics took him to the lofty position of Lord Chancellor. This status was short lived, however, because after only two years in office Bacon was prosecuted for taking bribes in his capacity as a judge. This was not an unusual occurrence in 17th-century England, in fact bribes were so widely available that judges could often afford to take them and ignore the wishes of those who gave them. Bacon claimed not to have been influenced by his receipt of bribes but was nonetheless fined, sentenced to imprisonment in the Tower of London and banished from public office on his release. Unable to pursue his political career, Bacon dedicated the rest of his life to philosophy.

FRANCIS BACON (1561–1626)

IN HIS ATTEMPT TO ESTABLISH A MORE PROGRESSIVE APPROACH TO PHILOSOPHY FRANCIS BACON SOUGHT TO CONNECT SCIENTIFIC REASON TO PRACTICAL CONCERNS FOR SCIENTIFIC RATIONALITY.

KNOWLEDGE IS POWER

Bacon was a champion of a movement opposed to the dominance of theology over scientific matters. The Renaissance had done much to weaken the authority of scholasticism but many people still needed converting to the values of scientific reason. In his attempt to convert the doubters, Bacon proposed, in *The New Atlantis*, an entirely new attitude to knowledge and methodology for the advancement of mankind. He argued that it is only through reason that men can hope to understand and control the laws of nature. Therein originates the famous maxim: 'Knowledge is power'. Therefore, even though reason can help religion (i.e. God's existence could be proved by reason) theology should be a separate discipline to philosophy. If there is a moral force to Bacon's philosophy, it is that philosophy should be driven by practical affairs rather than abstract moral speculation.

THE IDOLS

Bacon described the attitude he regarded as a hindrance to the advance of reason as the *'idols of knowledge'*. Idols are varieties of mental disposition which often steer us away from rational thought. There are four types of idol.

1. Idols of the tribe

This is our natural inclination to look for structures in nature which nature cannot offer us. Very often we invest our own hopes and desires in the understanding we have of nature and therefore tend to misread its laws.

2. Idols of the cave

This concerns the particular subjectivities of the person investigating nature, who is often swayed by his particular social background rather than the truth.

3. Idols of the marketplace

A tendency to use words which are too loosely defined and suitable to common language rather than scientific explanation. This is the idol which Bacon thinks most likely to halt or distract the advance of reason.

4. Idols of theatre

This is the grip that received doctrines like scholasticism have on human thought. They gain their strength from rhetoric rather than the truth.

Taken together the attitudes displayed in the four idols have characterised the social justification of science and indeed much philosophy to the present day.

INDUCTION

Bacon's own contribution to the cause of reason was an early version of empiricism (i.e. the theory that all statements depend for their truth on actual experience). He developed a theory of scientific induction, which suggested that in the pursuit of scientific knowledge one must employ the following methodology: firstly, one must search for instances where certain effects are inevitably caused by particular changes. Secondly, when we have found such an instance we must find all of the occasions which cause that particular effect. Then we must look for those instances where the particular change is not apparent and the effect is absent. Once we have exhausted these scenarios we can invent ways of measuring the logic of change and effect.

BELOW LEFT: APART FROM HIS PHILOSOPHICAL WORK BACON WROTE AN IMPORTANT HISTORY OF THE LIFE OF HENRY VII USING REVOLUTIONARY METHODS OF HISTORIOGRAPHY.

BELOW RIGHT: BACON BECAME EMBROILED IN AN ATTEMPTED COUP WITH THE EARL OF ESSEX.

"Knowledge and human power come to the same thing for nature cannot be conquered except by obeying her."

Thomas Hobbes is so important to political philosophy that the spectre of his uncompromising pronouncements on the fate of human communities continues to haunt political science to this day. His most famous work, *The Leviathan*, provided a view of the state and its relationship to the individual which is quintessentially modern in its conception of politics. Nonetheless, at the time of their publication his books met with almost universal condemnation.

HOBBES (1588–1679)

THE DISSIDENT PHILOSOPHER

After studying classics at Oxford, and a period as tutor to Lord Harwick, Hobbes travelled to Paris and Italy where he met Galileo. On his return to England in 1637 Hobbes was confronted by increasing social and political tension. England lapsed into civil war between Royalists, who Hobbes sided with, and Protestant parliamentarians. In 1640, and in the midst of executions of Royalists, Hobbes's sympathies led him to flee back to France where he continued his philosophical writings under protection by exiled Royalists. However, his position was a precarious one. In England his books were banned, not only for their Royalist slant but also for their apparent atheism, an unpopular quality with Royalists.

THE STATE OF NATURE

Hobbes begins his political theory with an account of the true nature of human beings. In nature, Hobbes argues, there is no truth, reason or justice. Such values are merely artificial attributes of human civilisation created by language and social convention. For Hobbes, without language there is no truth, and without truth there is no justice. In his natural state therefore, bereft of any knowledge of morality and justice, man lives in

'continual fear, and danger of violent death', because he has only his desire and instinct to guide him. The amoral struggle for survival that characterises man in his natural state reduces his life to a 'nasty, brutish and short' existence. To prove this, Hobbes says, one need look no further than the instinctual and egotistical nature of children before they are tamed by civilisation. This view of human nature was regarded as more radical when Hobbes was writing than it is today. In the early 17th century, most people believed that the absoluteness of God's will ensured that the forces of good and evil were present in all man's actions.

THE ABSOLUTE STATE

Hobbes offers human communities a stark choice in the face of the eternally egotistical foundation of human nature: we can either live under the violent and selfish shadow of human nature or give in to the necessity of a state with absolute and unlimited power which will bring relative harmony and comfort. To avoid living in constant fear a social contract is necessary; a contract between the individual and the select few who will hold the reigns of state power. The price to be paid for that solution is high: the power of those who command the instruments of state control must be unlimited.

THE LEGACY OF HOBBES

Hobbes's legacy is so powerful that political theory is yet to escape from the dichotomy of anarchy and order which comprised his justification of the state. Even the liberal tradition, which, in its most extreme, views the state as an evil to be controlled, is unable to break completely from the idea that without it there could be no democracy. In an age where nation state power is under constant threat, Hobbes's prescription is as relevant as ever. Furthermore, the establishment of international state authorities presents a renewed situation to which Hobbes's writings are particularly appropriate.

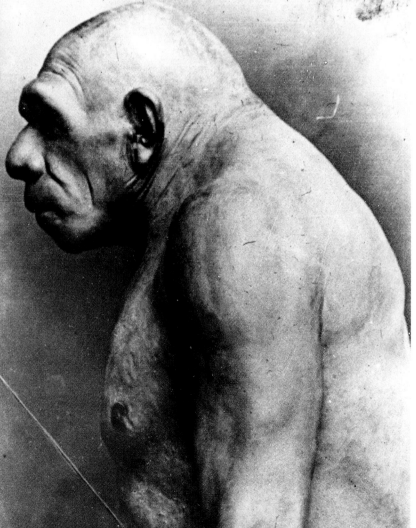

OPPOSITE PAGE: HOBBES'S BOOK *THE LEVIATHAN* CONTINUES TO POSE DIFFICULT QUESTIONS FOR POLITICAL PHILOSOPHERS.

ABOVE: HOBBES WAS FORCED TO FLEE ENGLAND DURING THE CIVIL WAR BETWEEN THE ROYALISTS AND PROTESTANT PARLIAMENTARIANS. HIS DEFENCE OF THE NECESSITY OF MAINTAINING A STRONG STATE GAVE HIS BOOKS A ROYALIST SLANT.

LEFT: HOBBES'S POLITICAL PHILOSOPHY WAS FOUNDED ON A CONCEPTION OF MAN IN HIS MOST NATURAL STATE, WHICH HE DESCRIBED AS BEING VIOLENT AND SELF-INTERESTED.

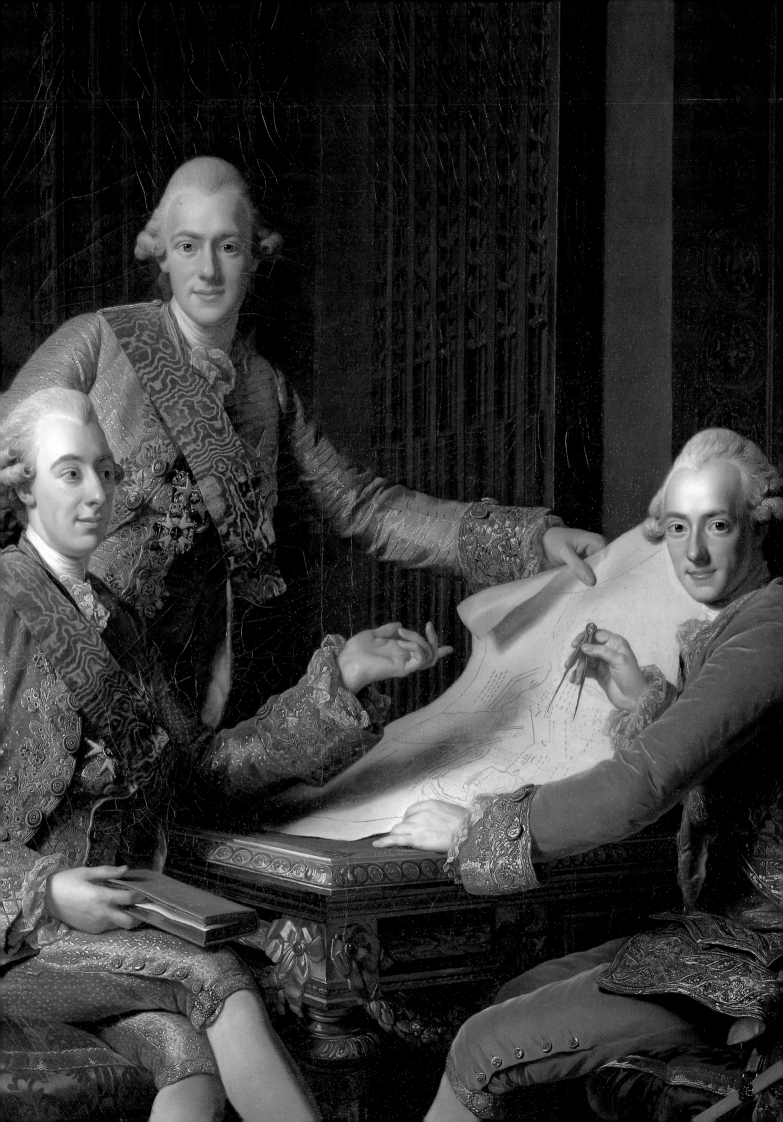

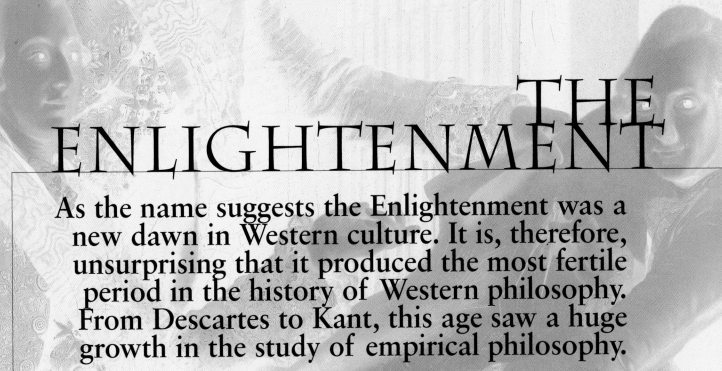

THE ENLIGHTENMENT

As the name suggests the Enlightenment was a new dawn in Western culture. It is, therefore, unsurprising that it produced the most fertile period in the history of Western philosophy. From Descartes to Kant, this age saw a huge growth in the study of empirical philosophy.

CHAPTER FIVE

The Enlightenment established a conflict between science and religion. For centuries European culture was dominated by religious practices; man's destiny was firmly placed in the hands of God. The scientific discoveries of the 17th and 18th centuries questioned the wisdom of this religious orthodoxy by establishing laws of nature which did not originate in divinity. Philosophy's contribution to this conflict was to take human destiny away from God and place it into the free will of man. However, many Enlightenment philosophers were also Christians and did not want to undermine religious belief completely. Their aim was to find a suitable place for religion which allowed science and rationality to advance without damaging the moral authority of Christianity. This was not an easy task and many protagonists of the Enlightenment suffered as a consequence.

THE AGE OF REASON

GALILEO

For centuries, scientific teaching combined religious belief and the logic and physics of Aristotle (the Greek master saw the world as a divinely ordained hierarchy). However the work of the Italian Galileo (1564–1642) literally turned science upside down. In *Dialogue on the Chief Systems of the World*, Galileo investigated the movements of the sun and the planets and developed Copernicus's theory that the sun revolves around the earth, rather than being static at the centre of the universe.

THE NEW DRIVE TO FIND APPLICATION FOR SCIENCE CAPTURED THE PUBLIC IMAGINATION AND HELPED PROMOTE THE NOTION THAT HUMAN KNOWLEDGE COULD BE ALL-SEEING.

From this investigation he developed a theory of motion which led to kinematics (the law of motion) and provided the basis for a science of dynamics. Galileo strongly believed that the 'laws of the natural world were firmly within the grasp of human rationality and not hidden in the hand of God'.

According to Galileo:

'*To pretend that truth is so deeply hidden from us and that it is hard to distinguish it from falsehood is quite preposterous: the truth remains hidden only while we have nothing but false opinions and doubtful speculations; but hardly has truth made its appearance than its light will dispel dark shadows.*'

Galileo's work was fiercely condemned and eventually the Pope found it necessary to intervene. Galileo was summoned to the Inquisition to answer for his 'heresy' on several occasions and he spent the last years of his life under arrest. The Catholic Church did eventually relent, granting him a posthumous pardon in the 20th century.

NEWTON

The scientific discoveries of Newton (1642–1727) did not receive the same condemnation as those of Galileo. The appreciation of Newton is clear from Alexander Pope's famous epitaph: 'Nature and Nature's laws lay hidden in night; God said, "Let Newton be!" and all was light.'

Newton was a remarkable scientist. His achievements were enormous, stretching from mathematics to the study of motion and the law of gravitation. Through Newton the laws of nature were firmly torn from the sacred doctrines in which they were previously captured. It is often said that Newton did more than any other man to force the tide of reason. The spirit of Enlightenment is commonly associated with his name.

DIVINE RIGHT AND DEMOCRACY

The English Revolution of 1688 was a turning point in the creation of the modern world. Through the revolution the Divine Right of Kings was challenged. The Revolution was a triumph for free will, the age of reason and the Enlightenment spirit. The secularism that characterised the age of reason had been translated into political power through the overthrow of the monarchy and the establishment of parliamentary sovereignty.

FRANCE AND THE PHILOSOPHES

France is widely designated as the intellectual and spiritual leader of the European Enlightenment. In the 18th century, French intellectuals led the way in promoting Enlightenment values, even though most of the key figures of the Enlightenment were not French. These intellectuals were commonly known as *The Philosophes* (the philosophers); Voltaire, Diderot and Montesquieu were the most famous. Their role was particularly significant, because France remained a Catholic state under the religious authority of Rome and so their battle against censorship and intolerance made them the martyrs of the Enlightenment. The most public expression of *The Philosophes'* promotion of Enlightenment was Diderot's *Encyclopedia*, which worked to bring rationalist philosophers together into a movement for Enlightenment. This movement expressed itself politically by pushing for reform of the law. Montesquieu, the political philosopher of the French Enlightenment, wrote a highly influential defence of republicanism entitled *The Spirit of the Laws*. He states his opposition to French monarchic rule: '. . . intelligent beings are capable of having laws that they have themselves made. To say that there is nothing just or unjust save that commanded or forbidden by existing laws is to say that before the circle was drawn not all its radii were equal.'

LITERATURE AND PHILOSOPHY

In Ancient Greece, the stories of Homer were a major source of philosophical inspiration, as

Alongside the celebrated philosophers of the Enlightenment (i.e. Descartes, Kant and Locke) were many, less famous, philosophers, artists and writers who made an essential contribution to the spreading of Enlightenment values. The work of these men and women helped create a climate fit for social and political change in late 18th century Europe.

VOICES OF REASON

ABOVE: THE FIRST ENCYCLOPEDIA WAS WRITTEN BY DIDEROT AND PUBLISHED IN 1752. IT WAS AN ENLIGHTENMENT INTERPRETATION OF THE PHYSICAL WORLD.

were the plays of Shakespeare to more recent philosophy. Philosophers, even the most systematic, rely on telling stories to elucidate their arguments. The clearest Enlightenment example of this fusion of philosophy and literature is in the philosophical tales of Voltaire. In his most widely read tale, *Candide*, Voltaire tells the story of a traveller who finds Enlightenment through his experiences whilst travelling. The story reflects Voltaire's commitment to a particular strand of the Enlightenment, empiricism (all knowledge derives directly from experience rather than any in-built rationality or higher authority). It is not only a great piece of Enlightenment propaganda, which promoted a practical, scientific philosophy, but also a satire on systematic philosophy which he regarded as necessarily contrary to real experience. However, Voltaire was by no means a secularist; as he famously said, 'If God did not exist, he would have to be invented.'

"So the philosopher who recognised a God has on his side a mass of probabilities which are equivalent to certainty, and the atheist has only doubts."

ABOVE: THE CAFÉS OF 18TH-CENTURY EUROPE WERE KEY VENUES FOR THE EXCHANGE OF SCIENTIFIC AND PHILOSOPHICAL IDEAS.
RIGHT: VOLTAIRE DID NOT DEVELOP A PARTICULARLY ORIGINAL PHILOSOPHY, BUT HE DID LEND HIS CONSIDERABLE LITERARY SKILLS TO THE CAUSE OF ENLIGHTENMENT.

René Descartes was a key figure in the intellectual revolution of 17th century Europe. Some argue that modern philosophy truly begins with Descartes.

RENÉ DESCARTES
(1596-1650)

René Descartes was a founding father of modern philosophy. His ideas were the first, and the most systematic, reflection of the early modern concern to view people as autonomous rational beings rather than beings whose fate is in the hands of a divine authority. Descartes signalled the decisive break in philosophy which had been gathering momentum under Hobbes and Bacon. Modern philosophy began with Descartes.

Descartes was born in a small town near Tours in France, the son of a landowner and councillor of the Parliament of Brittany. After studying at the Jesuit college of La Flêche in Anjou, Descartes travelled Europe, spending time in both the Dutch army and the Bavarian army. It was during his service in the Bavarian army that Descartes experienced the decisive moment in his life as a philosopher. On 10 November 1619, to escape from the cold weather, Descartes took shelter in a stove where he spent a day meditating. There he claims to have had a vision that persuaded him of the mission to which he should dedicate his life. That mission was to search for a completely new philosophical and scientific system of thought which would revolutionise our understanding of the fundamentals of human existence. It was a day which changed the course of philosophy.

DEMONS OF DOUBT

Descartes began his new philosophical system at the very beginning – with beliefs that were 'unquestionably certain'. Finding this beginning was not easy, however, because everywhere he looked Descartes was confronted with doubt – an evil demon of doubt which caused him to question the validity of the most basic beliefs. How for example, says Descartes, can I be sure that 'I am sitting here by the fire' when I know that I could be dreaming? Even more threatening to Descartes' sense of certainty was the possibility that there is a God who leads him astray every time he tries to perform the most basic mathematical calculation, such as two plus three. 'How do I know that these are not illusions that God has invented to trick me?'.

After considerable uncertainty about what it is possible to believe with certainty Descartes answers the demons of doubt that seemed to hinder his quest, stating:

'Let the demon deceive me as much as he may, he can never bring it about that I am nothing, so long as I think I am something…I am, I exist, is certain, as often as it is put forward by me or conceived in the mind'.

The one thing therefore of which he was certain is that 'I think therefore I am'. This is commonly known as Descartes' Cogito.

THE CARTESIAN SYSTEM

From this foundation Descartes proceeds to build his new philosophical system. He explains the foundation he has established and suggests that his certainty is justified because the idea is clear and distinct. It is not obscured by the senses and is based solely in the more reliable realm of the intellect. Emotion, subjective belief and other contingencies play no part in the realisation that 'I think therefore I am'. So in searching for clear and distinct ideas one must extinguish all elements of perception which derive from the senses, such as smell and sound. For Descartes, human rationality is founded upon a distinction between mind and body (often referred to in philosophy as mind–body dualism or Cartesian dualism). The mind, or the realm of the intellect, must contain innate ideas which are prior to experience, because it is experience which causes the demons of doubt.

Although Descartes' system marks a break in philosophy, the distinction between the senses and the intellect is inherited from antiquity. Both Plato and Aristotle had already developed forms of the distinction. In its original form Descartes' philosophy is now largely discredited. Few philosophers would now commit themselves to a rigid distinction between the mind and body and few would regard this as the foundation of human rationality. However, the idea that human beings have an inner core of unshakeable rationality is still very much alive. Additionally, Descartes' notion that a philosophy concerned with truth and certainty ought to be grounded in a concern to establish clear and distinct ideas remains the logic that drives much philosophy.

Baruch Spinoza was a product of the thriving intellectual atmosphere of 17th century Holland. Born and educated in Amsterdam, he was chastised for his apparently heretical beliefs and excommunicated by the Jewish community in which he grew up. However, he was still able to pursue philosophy by being a practising optician.

Spinoza's work can appear to be a confusing mixture of theology and philosophy. His work is very much a product of its age and does not easily fit into contemporary political philosophy. Spinoza represents the early Enlightenment attempt to break out, though not completely, from theology. Spinoza's contribution to Enlightenment philosophy owes much to Descartes. In terms of its celebration of human rationality it is less powerful and revolutionary than that of Descartes. However, as an attempt to develop an ethical and political theory from the new-found concern with rationality it is more important than Descartes and closer in its significance to Hobbes.

SPINOZA
(1632–77)

GOD AND EXISTENCE

Unlike Aristotle, Plato and indeed Descartes, Spinoza maintains that only one substance exists. That substance is God, which is infinite and universal. This is not a straightforward justification of received religious belief, because Spinoza does not believe that God's purposes can be broken down into good and evil. On the contrary, God has no specific purposes. Rather, God is simply the incarnation of everything; the universe is indivisible. The past, present and future are necessarily, but in another sense paradoxically, fixed. As he says, 'things could have been produced in no other way and in no other order'. Logically, one would think that human beings cannot have a free will, but Spinoza's *Ethics* allows for relative freedom of will.

> SPINOZA, LIKE MANY EARLY ENLIGHTEN-
> MENT THINKERS, WAS CONCERNED WITH
> THE RELATIONSHIP BETWEEN PHILOSOPHY
> AND THEOLOGY.

ETHICS

Spinoza's *Ethics* is based on two arguments: firstly, that human virtue is not a specific command of God and, secondly, that all human actions derive from the interest of self-preservation. There are two kinds of virtuous acts: first, pure self-preservation and, second, the virtue of friendship, which is always dictated by reason. Although there can be no other human motivation than self-preservation, that motivation will lead, if pursued rationally, to commonalities between men. For Spinoza, reason is self-preservation joined with understanding. Whilst self-preservation is absolute one can be neither virtuous or rational if one allows one's passions (interests derived from the senses) to control one's actions. This view of reason derives from Spinoza's understanding of human knowledge which is divided into three categories: sense perception, reason and intuitive knowledge.

POLITICAL THEORY

Spinoza's political theory is an important variation on Hobbes. Whereas Hobbes argued

that man is naturally selfish and competitive and therefore in need of complete subjugation to an absolute state, Spinoza argued that citizens can never actually give up their right to pursue their self-preservation. This is not for moral reasons but because the pursuit of self-preservation cannot be completely transferred to a state. The state's capacity to maintain its sovereignty depends upon its ability to determine the citizen's views of his own self-preservation. Unlike Hobbes, therefore, Spinoza suggests a more limited form of state power.

G.W. LEIBNIZ (1646-1716)

Leibniz's importance to the history of philosophy is not as obvious as that of Descartes, but the vast scope of his work certainly matches that of any of his contemporaries. In fact, he is widely regarded as one of the most intellectually impressive of all the great dead Western philosophers.

Gottfried Wilhelm von Leibniz was born the son of a Professor of Philosophy at the University of Leipzig. After receiving a doctorate at the University of Altdorf in 1663 he was successively employed as a librarian and a diplomat. His diplomatic tenure took him to both Paris and London where he became acquainted with the philosophy of Hobbes, Spinoza, Descartes and other eminent philosophers and scientists, whose work would not have been introduced to him at Altdorf. Leibniz led a fairly solitary existence, remaining unmarried throughout his life, which suited his intense character. However, he produced an enormous volume of work which went well beyond philosophy and into numerous areas of scientific investigation and mathematics. The sheer volume of Leibniz's contribution and the lack of a common thread running through his work, apart from a general Enlightenment spirit, make his work difficult to summarise.

THE PRINCIPLE OF SUFFICIENT REASON

According to Leibniz there is no inexplicable phenomenon. In other words, there must be a sufficient reason for why the world is the way it is. It cannot be the case that some phenomena are explicable and others not. If God has willed to deceive us, thus rendering human explanation uncertain, then he must have had a reason for his decision.

KEY CONCEPTS

Principle of non-contradiction

Leibniz's principle of non-contradiction asserts that the proposition 'a' and 'not a' cannot both be true. All propositions which are by implication contradictory or if in another sense denied resulting in a contradiction cannot be true.

"Truths of reason are necessary and their opposite is impossible: truths of fact are contingent and their opposite is possible."

God and humanity

One of the chief concerns of Enlightenment thinkers was the question of how to reconcile the human capacity for free will with the existence of God. If God created the world and is all powerful then he must have prior knowledge of future events. On the other hand if human beings are to be responsible for their decisions, which some would say is essential to a proper conception of justice, then surely God's influence on events must be limited, otherwise responsibility lies with God. But if we accept God's existence then, logically, we cannot accept any limitations on God's powers. Before the Enlightenment, Christian theological teaching, which dominated philosophical speculation, managed to uphold this dilemma through the doctrine of original sin. Leibniz believed that he could solve this dilemma in favour of the existence of both autonomous human rationality and an all-powerful God.

TOP: DURING HIS OWN LIFETIME LEIBNIZ WAS BEST KNOWN FOR HIS WORK ON MATHEMATICS AND THE DISCOVERY OF THE CALCULUS.
ABOVE: EVEN THOUGH HE WAS A THOROUGH RATIONALIST LEIBNIZ HAD A PASSION FOR ALCHEMY.

JOHN LOCKE
(1632–1704)

Locke's work is essential for those wishing to understand the construction of the modern liberal democratic state. An intellectual child of 17th century revolutionary England, Locke is viewed as the founder of modern Liberalism. As with Descartes', Locke's philosophy was a source of inspiration for Kant. However, his politics have outlived his philosophy.

Locke was born in Somerset, England, on 29 August 1632. His formal education began at Westminster School in 1645 and it is possible he witnessed the execution of Charles I in 1649. The execution of the king had a greater impact on his life than his years studying at Oxford University. He regarded the lectures and seminars as 'being invented for wrangling or ostentation rather than to discover truth'. He later became a physician to Lord Ashley, whose patronage also awarded him the post of secretary of presentations (director of church affairs in the office of the Lord Chancellor). After becoming embroiled by association in a conspiracy against the king, Locke fled to France until after the accession of William of Orange. Locke's philosophical career took off when he returned to England in 1690.

HUMAN UNDERSTANDING

In his book *An Essay on Human Understanding* (1671), Locke followed the custom of this era by explaining, in general terms, the path of human reason and its obstacles. He regarded himself as a practical philosopher and believed philosophy ought to be built upon reasoning and common sense rather than metaphysical speculation. Whether or not he achieves this aim is questionable, but his attempt was important to philosophy. While Descartes argued that knowledge, as opposed to mere opinion, stemmed from a set of clear and distinct ideas contained innately in the mind, Locke believed that our knowledge was not developed prior to experience. For Locke, the mind is a blank sheet of paper, upon which our experience is imprinted. Understanding is based not on something innate in our perception which causes us to know a fact when it confronts us, rather, our experience of the material world is filtered through ideas which we create to cope with it. Additionally, ideas are not absolute representations of our knowledge, because our knowledge is coloured by particular senses, such as sound, colour, etc.

In its intended form Locke's philosophy would not be accepted by contemporary philosophers. It is limited by its dependency on defining the exact relationship between our ideas and the natural workings of our mind; a relationship which is implied by Locke's thesis but also beyond the realm of human understanding because according to Locke we can only view the world through our impure ideas. Nonetheless, Locke's philosophy did become the first comprehensive exposition of empiricism, which subsequently became the foundation of the modern social sciences.

GOVERNMENT

Locke's initial concern was to create a political philosophy based on laws of nature which reason and experience suggests will provide the best practical policy for the governing human communities. He shares this concern with many of his contemporaries and predecessors alike. To do this, Locke set out to refute Hobbes's political philosophy, as Locke viewed this as providing justification for the Royalist cause he had worked against in the 17th century. Whereas Hobbes argued that in a state of nature, man's life is solitary and competitive and therefore in need of strong leadership, Locke argued that, in nature, man has a natural tendency to form contracts with his fellows for survival. Those contracts eventually take the form of moral laws. Whilst there is little doubt that a state authority is needed to protect those laws (e.g. the right to private property) any state that disregards man's natural inclination and right to preserve moral laws is working against nature and is thus regressive. For example, a monarchy which taxes a citizen's property without consent in the form of a universal contract, is contravening man's natural right to self-governance. In such a situation, citizens can legitimately repel the state's authority; an idea realised practically by the American revolutionaries' reaction to British imperial rule. The ideal relationship between the state and the citizens in civil society is a contractual one: constitutional government. The best form of government for Locke was one which consisted of a separation of powers between the legislature, the executive and the judiciary. This ensures man's natural rights are not abused by a government which is different only in name from a monarchy.

George Berkeley was one of a number of philosophers responsible for the emergence of a branch of philosophy called empiricism in the late 17th and 18th centuries. Though Berkeley's work has proved less durable than some of his contemporaries, his arguments are no less ingenious or interesting. The extravagance of much of his philosophy, which is responsible for its limited contemporary appeal, makes Berkeley's work all the more fascinating to the reader unaccustomed to the history of philosophy. The most striking of Berkeley's philosophical arguments is that matter or substances cannot be said to actually exist, independently of the mind.

GEORGE BERKELEY
(1685–1753)

BERKELEY (TOP) SUGGESTED THAT THE IMPRESSIONS WE GET FROM THE FIVE SENSES (THE PAINTING ABOVE SHOWS ABRAHAM GOVAERTS 16TH CENTURY INTERPRETATION OF THE SENSES) ARE NOT BASED ON ANY INNATE QUALITIES OF THE OBJECTS THAT OUR SENSES COME INTO CONTACT WITH. FOR EXAMPLE, ONE'S SENSE OF DISTANCE IS NOT CAUSED BY THE ACTUAL DISTANCE BETWEEN OBJECTS THEMSELVES.

BOUND FOR BERMUDA

Berkeley was born in Kilkenny, Ireland, in 1685. By the age of 22 he became a fellow of Trinity College, Dublin, where he had graduated three years earlier. It was during his fellowship at Trinity College, which lasted until 1724, that his most important philosophy was written. His most significant work, *The Dialogues of Hylas and Philonous*, was written in 1710. Believing that he had financial backing from the British government, Berkeley left Ireland in 1728 to go to Bermuda to educate the native Indians. When the money for his civilising mission failed to materialise, Berkeley returned to England and thereafter to Ireland where he became the Bishop of Cloyne in 1734. Away from philosophy, Berkeley is most remembered in California where a town is named after him.

HYLAS AND PHILONOUS

Berkeley's ideas are best understood in relation to those which were contended at the time he was writing. A great deal of his philosophy is concerned with challenging the most influential philosophical figures of the early 18th century – John Locke, René Descartes and the new science of Newton. The philosophical method made fashionable by Descartes was the starting point for Berkeley. This method entailed understanding what human knowledge could be known with certainty once all the scepticism one could muster was eradicated or dealt with. Berkeley's answer to the doubts one might muster is simply that only ideas, as perceived and created by the mind, can be known with any certainty.

Berkeley pursues this argument through the dialogue of two characters, Hylas and Philonous. Hylas represents the view of normal scientific common sense, whilst Philonous represents Berkeley's own views. Hylas begins the debate by criticising what he thinks are the unbelievable views of Philonous. 'Nothing', says Hylas, could be 'more fantastical, more repugnant to common sense...than to believe that there is no such thing as matter.' Philonous responds by arguing that, on the contrary, our understanding of what we

> "The chief thing I do or pretend to do is only to remove the mist or veil of words. This has occasioned ignorance and confusion. This has ruined the schoolmen and mathematicians, lawyers and divines."

regard to be actually existing objects or substances to which we attribute certain qualities, like white clouds or hot water, is an entirely mental affair. The objects or substances themselves do not force upon us, by the brute fact of their existence, the qualities we ascribe to them. Philonous goes on to use various examples to quash Hylas's understandable scepticism on this point. He begins with some obvious ones such as taste, pain and pleasure which he argues can have absolutely no basis in existence outside of the mind. He then moves on to more difficult subjects, e.g. colour. Can it be said that when an object appears to us as red that it contains

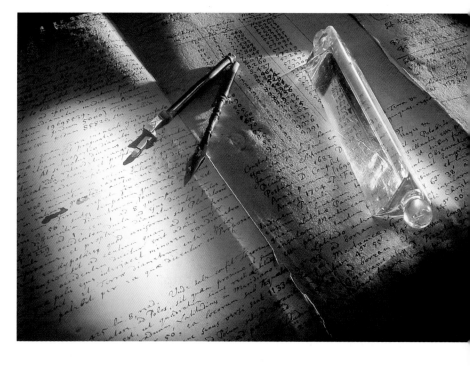

the necessary qualities of redness, despite our labelling it as red? For Berkeley the answer is quite simply no. The word red is merely a category and cannot actually exist in the colour. Apart from the obvious objection that there must be a natural phenomenon which causes us to believe that a table is red rather than blue, there are problems with Berkeley's philosophy. If we can only perceive ideas then how do we perceive the mind which must be accurately perceived in order to understand the status of ideas as described by Berkeley?

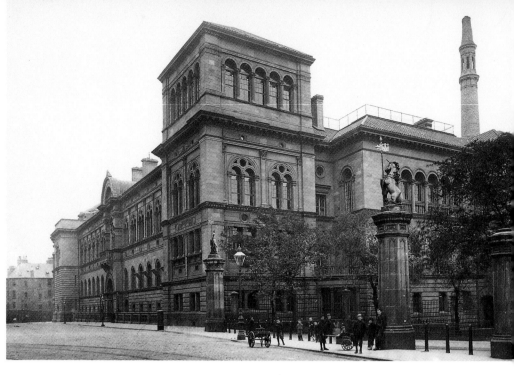

DAVID HUME (1711–76)

David Hume was born and educated in Edinburgh but produced his most important work, *A Treatise of Human Nature,* in France between 1734 and 1737. Hume served briefly as a military attaché and as a tutor before becoming secretary to Lord Hertford and the under-secretary of state for the Northern Department. He described himself as: '…a man of mild dispositions, of command of temper, of an open, social and cheerful humour, capable of attachment, but little susceptible of enmity, and of great moderation in all my passions'. Hume was an Enlightenment sceptic. Though he fully embraced the secular spirit of the Enlightenment (indeed more so than Descartes) he was sceptical about enthusiastic endorsements of human rationality, particularly by those claiming to have found the nature and limits of objectivity and truth. Hume's work contained the seeds of a counter-Enlightenment, although his scepticism did not deny the possibility of a constructive assessment of human nature and human virtue.

HUMAN NATURE

Hume believed that philosophy could not '…go beyond experience; and any hypothesis that pretends to discover the ultimate original qualities of human nature ought at first to be rejected as presumptuous and chimerical'.

This scepticism is based on Hume's claim that human perception, that is our capacity to make judgements about the world, originates in a distinction between 'impressions' and 'ideas'. *Impressions* have a more determinate grip on perception than *ideas* because they arise from the senses. The *impressions* we gain through our experience in the world via touch, sound, smell, taste and sight are the basis for our ideas. Those *ideas* are basically the perception of patterns in our experience. However, Hume admitted that he did not know the cause of human impressions in the mind.

'As to those impressions, which arise from the senses, their ultimate cause is, in my opinion, perfectly inexplicable by human reason, and will always be impossible to decide with

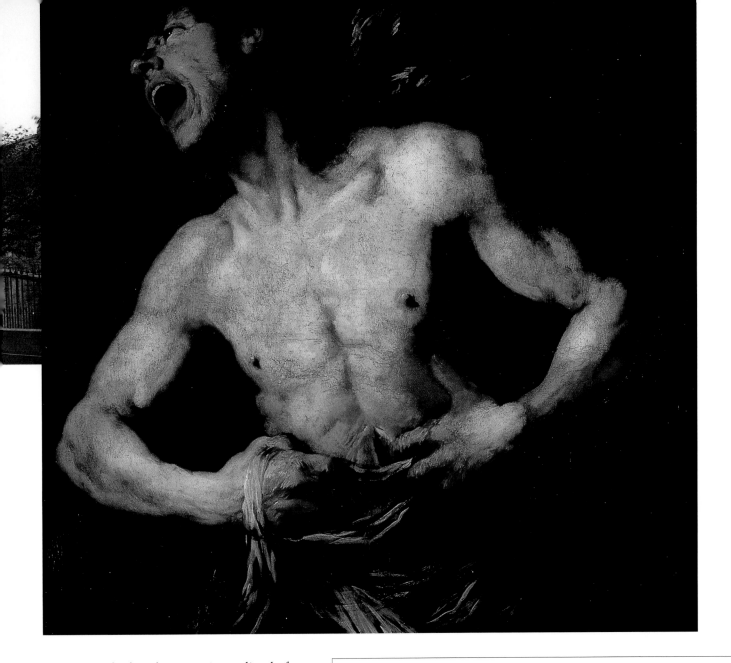

certainty, whether they arise immediately from the object, or are produc'd by the creative power of the mind, or are deriv'd from the author of our being.'

This quote indicates another important aspect of Hume's work: his theory of causal relation. According to this, there are no permanently necessary connections between different objects. The effects that we associate with a particular cause are simply a matter of consistency of experience. There are no external or natural laws that guarantee effects. Nonetheless, the assumption of cause and effect is essential to our existence.

MORAL REASON

In the spirit of Enlightenment secularism Hume understood morality as a wholly human construction, governed by human

HUME ARGUED THERE IS NO NECESSARY CONNECTION BETWEEN CAUSE AND EFFECT – EVEN WITH ELEMENTARY FEELINGS LIKE PAIN.

nature rather than a higher authority. In his account of human morality Hume follows Locke in rejecting Hobbes's argument that human beings are naturally selfish, violent and lonely creatures and stresses the communal disposition of human beings.

Hume's work has been overshadowed by Kant and Hegel, even though his arguments can be seen as a precipitated critique of Kant. After Hume's scepticism people might have been tempted to give up philosophy altogether. In fact, one reason for Kant's popularity is surely that he gave philosophers more to do and write about than Hume.

Kant provided a framework for philosophy from which it is yet to escape fully or replace with a successor. While Descartes is credited with establishing the foundations of modern philosophy, without Kant those foundations would have taken philosophy in a different direction. Kant guided philosophy in numerous directions, but most agree he provided a unifying force. After him, philosophy became autonomous, separate from science and theology and able to qualify the validity of claims made within both. Though it is impossible to give a permanent and uncontested definition of pure philosophy, Kant is the pure philosopher.

IMMANUEL KANT
(1724–1804)

TRANSCENDENTAL PHILOSOPHY

Descartes argued that the mind contains innate ideas prior to our experience, such as mathematical truths, but Kant disagreed. His philosophy begins with the modified premise that truths are transcended by philosophical arguments which explain them. He argued that, although our knowledge cannot completely transcend our experience, there is an essential structure to our knowledge which cannot be directly gained from experience (known as 'a priori knowledge'). The job of philosophy is to explain this structure. In *The Critique of Pure Reason*, Kant sets out to prove this and explain the structure which underpins our knowledge. He grants philosophy a special status: the Queen of the human sciences, above both science and history. To Kant, philosophy is the sovereign body of knowledge. Before this, all literary and scientific speculation was regarded as philosophy.

KANT IS WITHOUT DOUBT ONE OF THE MOST IMPORTANT EUROPEAN PHILOSOPHERS. HE CHALLENGED MUCH OF THE WORK OF EARLIER ENLIGHTENMENT THINKERS AND LAID THE FOUNDATIONS FOR THE NEXT WAVE OF EUROPEAN THINKERS.

JUDGEMENT

Kant developed a theory of human judgement in his efforts to explain the structure which underpins human knowledge. He argued that there are two types of human judgement, analytic and synthetic. Analytic judgements are validated for truthfulness simply by understanding the terms given in the statement that makes them up. For example, the statement 'all bachelors are unmarried' is true whatever our experience, because the meaning of 'unmarried' is contained wholly in the term 'bachelors'. The statement is therefore *a priori* knowledge. Synthetic judgements, however, require extended proof of their validity. For example, the statement 'all bachelors do not want to be married' is 'synthetic' because we cannot be certain without empirical investigation of the desires of all bachelors. The distinction between analytic and synthetic judgements is the foundation of Kant's transcendental philosophy. Thereafter his theory becomes considerably more complex. At first glance, the distinction may appear to be obvious, but its importance to philosophy is considerable. This is because if one denies that *a priori knowledge* exists or is impossible to understand then one must be open to the possibility that human beings can never be certain of truth when presented with it.

However, Kant's transcendental philosophy has now become eminently questionable, especially after recent philosophical speculation. Kant does not prove the existence of *a priori* knowledge, rather he simply defines certain accepted linguistic practices. This is an issue of considerable controversy in contemporary philosophy. Some argue that, since our values of justice depend on the belief that truth is attainable, this view is socially very damaging.

THE MORAL IMPERATIVE

Kant's moral philosophy begins with the premise that the foundation of all moral reason is man's ability to act rationally. He argues that it is only man that has the ability to act above instinct and self-interest. For Kant, a virtuous act is not an indication of a virtuous person, because strictly speaking animals are able to act virtuously. It is true that virtue must be based on the idea of law, because law transcends particular acts. Law in turn should be based on the autonomous rationality of human beings who should be viewed as ends in themselves rather than beings who are pre-judged by a particular moral order. Therefore, justice exists in the fairness of procedure as opposed to forces external to human rationality. In recent years this view has been hotly contested. It has been argued that human rationality is thoroughly communal and that the neglect of this fact only promotes undesirable individualism.

THE KANTIAN TRADITION

There are two types of Kantian tradition – one explicit and one implicit. The implicit one believes, as Kant did, that philosophy's job is to develop a theory of knowledge but it also believes that Kant had taken the wrong route through transcendentalism. The more explicit Kantian tradition attempts to develop Kant's original thesis. This tradition now shows itself in political philosophy and mainly through the works of John Rawls and Jürgen Habermas.

THE HUMAN BRAIN: BY ARGUING THAT PURE REASON DOES NOT HAVE TO DEPEND UPON A PARTICULAR COURSE OF EXPERIENCES FOR ITS RATIONALISING, IMMANUEL KANT TRANSFORMED THE WAY IN WHICH MODERN ACADEMICS STUDIED HUMAN RATIONALITY.

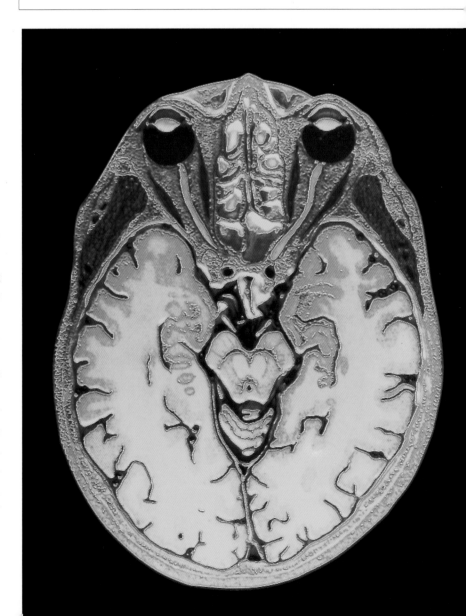

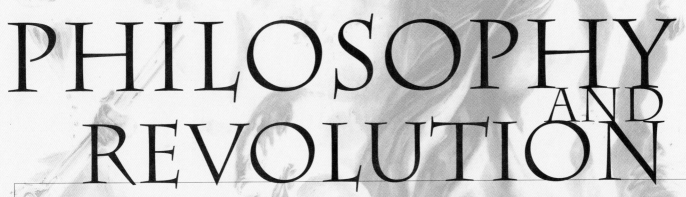

PHILOSOPHY AND REVOLUTION

Philosophy is a fundamental ingredient in revolution. The work of thinkers such as Paine and Marx has provided the ideological foundation for rapid political change. Without this intellectual ammunition the modern world would be a very different place.

CHAPTER SIX

The French Revolution of 1789 represents a point of departure for modern European civilisation. Modern conceptions of nation, citizenship, radicalism, equality and democracy were born out of the intellectual climate of the Revolution. The hopes and ideas of European politics and philosophy are enacted within the story of the Revolution and its lessons are still being understood. For this reason, the French Revolution was a fertile ground for philosophical speculation about social and political change. Many philosophical traditions would be inconceivable had the French Revolution never occurred.

THE FRENCH REVOLUTION

LOUIS XIV WAS GUILLOTINED IN 1793. HIS LAST WORDS WERE: 'I HOPE THAT MY BLOOD MAY SECURE THE HAPPINESS OF THE FRENCH PEOPLE.'

THE RIGHTS OF MAN AND CITIZEN

The Declaration of the Rights of Man and Citizen by the newly established Assembly on 26 August 1789 is a key moment in the history of philosophy. The writers of the Declaration were exposed to conflicting pressures. As representatives of the French bourgeoisie they were concerned that the system which replaced the old feudal rule was able to protect property rights through law. However, popular revolutionary fervour, driven by the propertyless and the poor, wanted much more than rights to property. It demanded that popular will was enshrined in the new institutions. The members of the Assembly combined the interests of security and property, with the question of sovereignty and citizenship, by declaring that 'sovereignty rests in the nation' and that the will of the nation would be embodied in the actions of its representatives. In the 18th and 19th centuries the term

democracy became synonymous with the idea of popular sovereignty as expressed in the French Revolution. This idea took on more acute forms under the populist patriotism of Maximilien Robespierre after the second revolution in 1792. The French Revolution ensured that, thereafter, European politics was dominated by the problem of reconciling the spirit of popular sovereignty with the need for effective and strong government.

THE TERROR OF REVOLUTION

Many philosophical questions which emerged out of the French Revolution concerned the explanations given for the Reign of Terror that engulfed France after the second revolution. It was argued, by some, that the Reign of Terror was an example of the dangers of the democratic spirit. According to this theory, if the democratic spirit is taken to its logical conclusion the result is a tyranny of the majority. Whatever the cause, terror was certainly the outcome of the post-revolutionary period in France. This led to speculation that in times of radical change the need to consolidate power can become more important than the principles which that power seeks to advance.

ABOVE: ROBESPIERRE (1758-94), THE FRENCH REVOLUTIONARY LEADER, TOOK THE IDEAS OF POPULAR SOVEREIGNTY TO THEIR EXTREMES.
BELOW: THE STORMING OF THE BASTILLE IN JULY 1789 HAS BEEN TAKEN TO SIGNIFY THE START OF THE FRENCH REVOLUTION.

THE AMERICAN REVOLUTION

If we define a revolution to be a violent struggle against the state followed by widespread social and political upheaval then the American Revolution was no revolution at all. It was essentially a war of independence against Britain. The expectations of the revolutionaries were modest. Many participants in the events of 1776 did not hope to create a Utopia, and the Revolution did not result in the kind of upheaval which later occurred as a result of the Russian Revolution in 1917. There was no redistribution of wealth or attempt to install new moral values. The revolutionary quality of the American Revolution was encapsulated in the creation of a new kind of state. The constitutional government created after the Declaration of Independence from Britain in 1776 was the practical realisation of much Enlightenment philosophy. As George Washington remarked, the Revolution 'laid open for us…the treasures of knowledge acquired by labours of philosophers, sages and legislators through a long succession of years'. The relationship between state and society established by the constitution became the backdrop to much philosophical speculation thereafter.

ABOVE: THE BOSTON TEA PARTY WAS A PIVOTAL EVENT IN THE RISE OF ANTI-BRITISH FERVOUR.
RIGHT: THOMAS JEFFERSON (1743-1826) WAS THE LEADING INTELLECTUAL FIGURE OF THE AMERICAN REVOLUTION.

THE REVOLUTION AND ITS LEADERS

After a series of arbitrary decrees from the British government the American colonists, under the leadership of George Washington and the Continental Congress, established an army with French help which eventually defeated the British in 1781. However, five years earlier the colonists made the all important Declaration of Independence. The key figure behind the Declaration of Independence was Thomas Jefferson, whose *Defence of Liberty and the Rights of Man* was the intellectual force behind the Revolution. The following passage from the Declaration indicates Jefferson's revolutionary beliefs:

'We hold these truths to be self-evident, that all men are created equal, that they are endowed by their Creator with certain unalienable Rights, that among these are Life, Liberty and the pursuit of Happiness... That whenever any Form of Government becomes destructive of these ends, it is the Right of the People to alter or to abolish it, and to institute new Government, laying its foundation on such principles and organizing its powers in such form, as to them shall seem most likely to effect their Safety and Happiness.'

This political philosophy, inspired by Locke and Paine, became the foundation of a new republic. The spirit of the Revolution was not driven by dreams of democracy, but by more important concerns of security and freedom. However, the aims and ideals of the American revolutionaries were limited.

STATE AND SOCIETY

The writers of the Constitution had to overcome a number of difficult and conflicting issues. Chief among these was how to ensure freedom without resorting to the creation of an over-powerful state to protect it. The experience of British rule had made the revolutionaries aware of the dangers of arbitrary rule, but without a strong state how could newly independent America protect itself from the threat of further foreign intervention? This question caused great debate amongst the Founding Fathers of the Constitution. A compromise was eventually reached and ultimate sovereignty was invested in the people, but by limiting the power of the state such sovereignty could never be thoroughly enacted. The Constitution was eventually ratified in 1788.

THE IDEA OF AMERICA

For many philosophers America is much more than a country, it is an idea. It represents the ideals which spearheaded the Enlightenment, in their most acute form.

No writer made a more powerful intellectual contribution to the revolutions of the late 18th century than Tom Paine. In that regard, his contribution to modern political philosophy is unparalleled. The revolutions in America and France were more than critical moments in history, they were the birth-places of modern politics. These revolutions led to the modern concepts of nation, human rights, citizenship and constitutional government. Paine's enormous contribution to both revolutions widens the significance of his work beyond philosophy. Above all else Paine stands as a champion of the liberties of the ordinary citizen against power-hungry states and therefore speaks to the contemporary world as much as the world of the 18th century.

THOMAS PAINE
(1737–1809)

THE REVOLUTIONARY CITIZEN

Paine was born in Thetford, England, the son of a Quaker, and it was his father's values which sowed the seeds of his concern with the welfare of ordinary and underprivileged people. Paine's revolutionary life did not start until he was into his late thirties, although his sensitivity to state corruption was awakened earlier during his service as an excise collector.

In 1774, after spending time in London where he became acquainted with the new scientific reasoning of the age, Paine set off to America. His arrival coincided with growing discontent about the arbitrariness of the British government's intervention in the lives of Americans. Paine helped to channel this discontent into words through his editorship of *The Pennsylvania Magazine*. However, his most profound contribution to the growing revolutionary fervour was *Common Sense*, which sold over 150,000 copies in America alone (an unprecedented success in the 18th century). Once British imperial rule had been removed and the job of building a constitution became the main concern, Paine moved back to England. In 1791, two years after the storming of the Bastille and the French Revolution,

Paine published a defence of the virtues of revolution called *The Rights of Man*, which was to become the best-selling book of the day, selling over 250,000 copies in two years in England alone. Its crisp, plain use of language marked it out against other revolutionary literature of the time.

COMMON SENSE

The object of Paine's scorn in *Common Sense* was monarchy, and in particular the British monarchy. The Glorious Revolution of 1688 had failed, according to Paine, to control the in-built potential for the abuse of power which was a characteristic of monarchic rule. Paine, thought that though 'we have been wise enough to shut and lock the door against absolute monarchy, we at the same time have been foolish enough to put the Crown in

ABOVE: MAD TOM, OR MAN OF RIGHTS. PAINE'S FAME MADE HIM A PRIME TARGET FOR RIDICULE. DESPITE HIS DEFENCE OF THE REVOLUTION HE WAS IMPRISONED FOR HIS ATTATCHMENTS TO A POLITICAL FACTION.

possession of the key'. Paine's hatred of the monarchy resulted in his vilification of the absurdity of monarchic rule. According to Paine, monarchies necessarily rule by institutionalising their ignorance of the world through their detachment from it. For Paine, the irrationality of monarchy was one of many reasons why citizens should resist it. He believed citizens had the right to live in a society which valued liberty above the folly of much tradition, a right which Paine thought could be grasped by American people; a sentiment expressed in his famous rallying call prior to the American Revolution: 'O! ye that love mankind! Ye that dare oppose not only tyranny but the tyrant, stand forth!'

THE RIGHTS OF MAN

In response to Edmund Burke's attack on the dangers of revolution, Paine continued his

> **"It is impossible that such governments as have hitherto existed in the world, could have commenced by any other means than a total violation of every principle sacred and moral."**

attack on the monarchic abuse of power: 'The idea of hereditary legislators is as inconsistent as that of hereditary judges, or hereditary juries, and as absurd as an hereditary mathematician, or an hereditary wise man.' Against the claims of traditionalists like Burke who believed in ordered hierarchical societies, Paine believed that human beings had inalienable natural rights. The primary function of the state is to protect these rights, which is why, according to Paine, we must view the state as a necessary evil. However, Paine had a more significant role in mind for the state than his fear of state power implied. His concern for the ordinary citizen led him to conceive the first comprehensive system of welfare protection, which would alleviate the condition of the European masses which gave rise to the French Revolution.

There are few political philosophers who reacted against the Age of Reason and its revolutionary upheaval who are also regarded as relevant to modern issues. Edmund Burke is one such philosopher. His work was a product of the political climate at the time of the French Revolution, but it also has a contemporary significance. Burke's writings constitute the intellectual beginnings of modern Conservatism, represented most clearly today by the British Conservative Party.

EDMUND BURKE (1729–97)

DUBLIN TO LONDON

Edmund Burke was born in Dublin in 1729. He moved to London to study law and from 1765 to 1794 he sat as a member of the House of Commons. His description of the role of Members of Parliament remains a key work for those trying to understand British parliamentary democracy.

REFLECTIONS ON REVOLUTION

Burke's 1790 publication *Reflections on the Revolution in France* was widely acclaimed for its attack on the political principles of the passionate French revolutionaries. This view appealed to the English ruling classes who feared that revolutionary fervour might spread across the Channel. Those who shared this view were quick to lay praise on Burke's book.

Burke criticised the revolutionaries' blind pursuit of abstract principles and argued that their natural rights philosophy ignored reality. According to Burke, relations between people are purely artificial and political contracts are established on tradition and custom rather than natural rights or equality. There is no politically meaningful natural equality and efforts to enforce this ideal are dangerous: 'Government is not made in virtue of natural rights, which may exist in total independence of it; and exist in much greater clearness, and in a much greater degree of abstract perfection: but their abstract perfection is their practical defeat.'

Burke argued that governments guided by pragmatism are much more adaptable and can react appropriately and more quickly to particular situations than governments guided by principles held dogmatically or established as eternally justified. Moreover, the unwritten British constitution can preserve both that which is good in tradition and that which is desirable in new ideas. 'Besides, the people of England well know, that the idea of inheritance furnishes a sure principle of conservation, and a sure principle of transmission; without at all excluding a principle of improvement. It leaves acquisition free; but it secures what it acquires...locked fast as in a sort of family settlement.'

THE ORGANIC SOCIETY
Burke describes the society which best reflects the way in which social and political relationships are inevitably built on tradition as the 'organic society'. An organic society functions

like a human body, with all its parts carrying out their functions. Such a society creates a '...habitual social discipline, in which the wiser, the more expert, and the more opulent conduct, and by conducting enlighten and protect, the weaker, the less knowing, and the less provided with the goods of fortune'.

BURKE AND MODERN CONSERVATISM
Burke is the intellectual father of modern Conservatism. His beliefs in tradition, pragmatism and an organic society became the three pillars of traditional Conservatism. Even though the type of Conservatism Burke favoured is less fashionable now, the success of his ideas, as transmitted through the British Conservative Party, is widely regarded as a key factor in the lack of revolutionary upheaval in Britain compared with the rest of Europe.

ABOVE: IN WRITING A CRITIQUE OF THE REVOLUTION IN FRANCE, BURKE PRODUCED THE MOST POWERFUL DEFENCE OF THE BRITISH SYSTEM OF GOVERNMENT EVER WRITTEN. OVER 200 YEARS LATER, THE PRINCIPLES WHICH BURKE OUTLINED CONTINUE TO INFORM BRITISH PARLIAMENTARY DEMOCRACY. LEFT: IN 18TH CENTURY BRITAIN, POLITICAL SATIRE WAS PARTICULARLY VENOMOUS AND BURKE WAS THE SUBJECT OF GREAT RIDICULE.

Rousseau is a particularly difficult thinker to categorise, his writing has been variously described as romantic, liberal and totalitarian. His work challenged the received doctrine of social and political philosophy. He was the first philosopher to question the bracketing of moral and political ideas which had taken shape in the 18th century. More than 200 years later, Rousseau's philosophy remains resistant to attempts to classify it. However, this cannot diminish the influence he had upon 18th century European thought nor his impact upon subsequent political philosophy. No lesser figure than Kant described him as the Newton of the moral world.

JEAN JACQUES ROUSSEAU (1712–78)

ROUSSEAU WAS THE MOST NOTORIOUS OF THE 18TH-CENTURY FRENCH PHILOSOPHERS. IN 1762 HE FLED FRANCE WHEN HIS BOOK EMILE WAS CONDEMNED BY PARLIAMENT.

Rousseau was the first thinker to question the Age of Reason without defending the religious authority which the age threatened. He stood outside the circle of the enlightened French *philosophes* and the *Encyclopedia* which brought them together but he was not simply an irrationalist. Edmund Burke, the famous 18th century Conservative, described Rousseau as the most acute incarnation of the Age of Reason. His popularity as a political philosopher was not based on the rational force of his arguments but on his appeal to an impossibly Utopian future and the idyllic depiction of life before reason. This is the reason why Rousseau is sometimes described as a Romantic.

Rousseau was born in Geneva in 1712, and orphaned at the age of ten. He lived with an aunt until he was 16, when he impulsively left Geneva. After neglecting to keep track of the time on an evening walk in the country, Rousseau returned to the city gates to find they had been closed. On previous occasions he had waited until the morning to enter the city, but this time his spirit of adventure persuaded him not to go back. He travelled to Turin where he converted to Catholicism. He eventually settled in France where he spent several years as a musician. His philosophy career began when he won a literary prize for an essay in response to the question: 'Has the revival of the arts and sciences done more to corrupt or purify morals?' His answer, in short, was that it had corrupted human morality. This essay, and others which followed, associated Rousseau with ideals that celebrated the natural inclinations of man.

Rousseau argued, in his *Discourse on Inequality*, that man had not achieved greater happiness through modern civilisation, as man's happiness is contained in all the things he has in a 'state of nature'. What Rousseau meant by 'a state of nature' was not human instincts in isolation, but man in the state of nature before man had created civil society. His depiction of nature was a romantic synthesis of propertyless communal life and passionate egoism – man in his most perfect idyllic state.

THE GENERAL WILL

The first line of Chapter One of Rousseau's *The Social Contract* reads, 'Man was born free, and he is everywhere in chains.' Rousseau criticised the modern concern to discover the most legitimate form of force which men could use to set themselves free. According to Rousseau, men cannot have freedom simply by yielding to force. 'Force is physical power; I do not see how its effects can produce morality. To yield to force is an act of necessity not of will; it is at best an act of prudence. In what sense can it be a moral duty?' In *The Social Contract*, Rousseau attempts to conceive an ideal society which is neither driven by a particular interest, such as the protection of property, nor neglectful of such interest. 'The problem,' according to Rousseau, 'is to find a form of association which will defend and protect with the whole common force the person and goods of each associate, and in which each, while uniting himself with all, may still obey himself alone, and remain as free as before.' In doing so he attempted to square the great modern political conflict between liberty and equality. He argued there is an objective general interest, which is so objective and absolute that at the same time it is the most objective expression of self-interest. He calls this interest the 'general will'. Rousseau was vague about how and when the general will could be realised.

Rousseau's philosophy is filled with paradoxes, but any inconsistency or apparent contradiction is no oversight. Throughout *The Social Contract* Rousseau juggles concepts of 'the particular' and 'the universal'. For Rousseau these paradoxes are necessary ingredients of modern thought and progress requires us to reconcile them. Critics have been keen to point out the dangers of his philosophy. In particular, commentators have noted the danger of arbitrary definitions of the general will, for instance those leaders who claim to express the general will and believe themselves justified in enforcing it with coercion. Nonetheless, the problem of reconciling liberty and equality continues to overwhelm political philosophy.

FAR LEFT: ROUSSEAU IS OFTEN REFERRED TO AS HAVING LAID THE INTELLECTUAL FOUNDATIONS OF THE FRENCH REVOLUTION, PARTICULARLY HIS THEORY THAT FREEDOM COULD ONLY BE ACHIEVED THROUGH THE ENFORCEMENT OF THE GENERAL WILL.
LEFT: IN THE OPENING TO HIS BOOK *THE SOCIAL CONTRACT* ROUSSEAU FAMOUSLY WROTE 'MAN WAS BORN FREE, AND HE IS EVERYWHERE IN CHAINS.'

FRANKENSTEIN'S FOREBEAR

Born in 1756, in Hoxton, near London, Godwin rejected the Calvinism of his parents, which had produced so many other important intellectual figures of his time. During the 1780s Godwin mingled with the radical intellectuals of Soho in London. He made his way as an ad hoc journalist and writer until the French Revolution concentrated his mind on questions of justice, liberty and revolution. Two years after the French Revolution he began work on his most important work: *Enquiry Concerning Political Justice*, which was published in 1793. Despite his strong views against the institution of marriage, Godwin married the radical feminist Mary Wollstonecraft (author of *A Vindication of the Rights of Women*) after she became pregnant. Mary died 10 days after giving birth. Their daughter, also called Mary, went on to marry the English poet Shelley (from whom Godwin had borrowed money to sustain his philosophical activities and his position as a lone parent). Mary Godwin Shelley later became famous for writing the novel Frankenstein, the philosophical inclination of which owed considerable debt to her father.

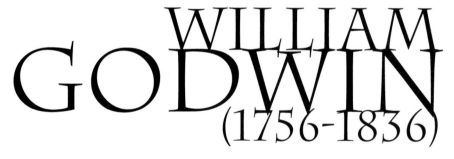

WILLIAM GODWIN (1756-1836)

Known in 18th century London as simply 'The Philosopher', William Godwin gave the most comprehensive treatise on Anarchism ever produced. However, most of his contemporaries understood him merely as a radical – as a philosopher of justice and happiness. To the circle of radical intellectuals in London at the time, Godwin's writing stood out as having the most depth and philosophical credibility. The young English poet Coleridge wrote a sonnet to Godwin, indicating the esteem in which he was held:

And hum thee, Godwin! With ardent lay!
For that thy voice, in passions stormy day
When wild I roamed the blacheath of distress
Bade the bright form of justice meet my way
And told me that her name was happiness.

EVIL GOVERNMENT

Like the philosopher Jean Jacques Rousseau, Godwin was severely critical of the political tradition of Hobbes and Locke, which had dominated issues of justice and government. Rousseau contended that man has no natural rights beyond those which are for the good of a particular community. However, Godwin came to quite different conclusions to other philosophers whose views were based on this anti-liberal stance. Instead of favouring a government which seeks justice for the whole above the individual. Godwin argued that 'Government is, in all cases, an evil; it ought to be introduced as sparingly as possible. Man is a species of being whose excellence depends on his individuality; and who can be neither great nor wise, but in proportion as he is independent.'

For Godwin, governments are upheld by ignorance. Knowledge, truth and reason must always be given a higher value than the law. In practice, law is either enforced for a particular interest, or simply because it exists. It is less interested in the truth or reason than it is in its own application. Godwin applies similar scorn to the institutions that create and apply the law. Political and social institutions are surrounded by mystery and complexity; this is not because reason and truth are particularly difficult to understand, but because it is necessary to dupe citizens about the irrationality of the government's activities and the interests that lie behind them.

COMMUNITY WITHOUT LAW

The utopia that Godwin imagines instead of government places a considerable demand upon human nature. Godwin's ideal of the perfect society consisted of a kind of self-governing, parish community. The community would have no need for law at all, or any of the bureaucracy of state. When a particular dispute was brought to light, a jury would be established solely to consider it so that the interests of truth and justice could be secured above those of any law. Godwin's parish community would essentially be held together by the sincerity of its citizens.

THE MOST POPULAR REFLECTIONS OF ANARCHIST IDEAS OCCURRED DURING THE SPANISH CIVIL WAR (1936-39), WHERE VARIOUS ANARCHIST GROUPS PLAYED AN IMPORTANT, ALBEIT FRACTUOUS, PART IN THE FIGHT AGAINST FRANCO AND FASCISM.

The significance of the philosophy of Karl Marx is immense. In his name, the world has been transformed. However, his fame is such that he is more often cited than read. Marx was born in Treves, Germany, in 1818, and after attending university he worked as a journalist in Paris, Cologne and Brussels. He also participated in the 1848 revolutions in France and Germany, after which he moved to London. Whilst in London he met Friedrich Engels, a factory manager from Manchester, with whom he was later to publish *The Communist Manifesto*. Engels introduced Marx to the conditions of British workers as well as classical theories of economics. While he was in London, working mostly in the British Library, Marx wrote his most famous work, *Das Capital*.

KARL MARX (1818–1883)

THE HUMAN CONDITION

The starting point for Marx's philosophy is the relationship between man and the world he creates. For Marx, the logic of all human history and human relationships is constituted by that which man creates from his environment. Man's productivity is the origin of all history, therefore labour is essential to man and any community he forms. According to Marx labour is 'the everlasting nature-imposed condition of human existence, and therefore is independent of every social phase of that existence, or rather, is common to every such phase'. Marx rejected the work of philosophers who had tried to provide a static definition of human nature. The only permanent ingredient of human nature, according to Marx, is its inclination towards productivity, otherwise human nature is as malleable as history is continuous. This led Marx to develop his theory of 'historical materialism'.

HISTORICAL MATERIALISM

Marx believed that history is guided by the material conditions within which men live. These conditions are, in turn, determined by the economic structures which are constructed around the forms of productivity within which

Marx's influence as a philosopher is so great that it is impossible to account for. However, his philosophy is invoked much more than it is read or understood.

men are engaged. The kind of life a man leads is therefore determined by the position he has in the productive relationships that society has created. This view of society is also known as 'economic determinism'. All human phenomena can be understood through economics.

HISTORY AND THE CLASS STRUGGLE

From the premise that all human history is materially determined, Marx went on to explain the particular development of human history. He argued that there are essentially three stages of human history: Feudalism, Capitalism and finally Communism. All three are born out of class struggles. In each phase one class dominates, and is in conflict with, another. It is these conflicts which determine the social and economic structures of that society. The English Revolution, for example, which brought about the dismantling of

is the way value is attached to goods and labour in Capitalist societies. Marx believed that the act of exchange within the Capitalist system was separate from the use-value of things. The factor which actually determines the value of things is the quantity of labour needed to produce them. This law is so pervasive under Capitalism that it also applies to the labourer, who is given a particular value according to his productive potential. In the Capitalist system, there is a contradiction between the value attached to the labourer's productivity and the worth of the goods he produces. Marx believed that once the proletariat realised the inherent contradictions of Capitalism they would spontaneously overthrow the system. He also believed that Britain and Germany, the most advanced Capitalist societies in the mid-19th century, would be first to experience revolution.

Feudalism was a product of conflict between the emerging bourgeoisie and the old land-owners. Marx thought Capitalism contained contradictions which would eventually lead to its demise. Chief among these contradictions

MARX'S MAMMOTH WORK, *DAS KAPITAL*, WAS FAMOUSLY WRITTEN IN THE READING ROOMS OF THE BRITISH LIBRARY IN LONDON.

PIERRE JOSEPH PROUDHON
(1809–65)

Pierre Joseph Proudhon was the first political philosopher to call himself an Anarchist philosopher. His humble background (his parents were born peasants) drove Proudhon to pour scorn on the decadence and luxury of the metropolis which controlled peasant labour. Proudhon mixed this attitude with the puritanical outlook typical of the provincial French working class. Proudhon's mistrust and resentment of authority is reflected in the fact that he was entirely self-educated. His

political pamphlets, books, articles, his practical rejection of authority, and his participation in the 1848 wave of revolution in Europe made him famous. He also began the quarrel between Karl Marx and the Anarchists in the 1840s and 50s. Although Marx was also a radical he was as much Proudhon's enemy as the ruling elite in France. In response to Marx's request that they work together he wrote: 'after abolishing all *a priori* dogmatisms, do not let us dream of indoctrinating the people in our turn; do not let us fall into the contradiction of your compatriot Luther, who, after overthrowing the Catholic theology, at once began, armed with excommunications and anathemas, to found Protestant theology'.

A CARTOON DEPICTING PROUDHON BEING ABDUCTED BY AMERICANS SHOWS HOW UNPOPULAR HIS IDEAS WERE WITH SOME PEOPLE.

PROPERTY IS THEFT!

Proudhon's most acclaimed book, published in 1842, was entitled *What is Property?* His famous answer to this question was 'property is theft!' Proudhon believed no man has an eternal right to property. He also stated that property inevitably leads to tyranny, because it is chiefly through property that the mass of people are subject to slavery through labour.

VIOLENCE AND REVOLUTION

Liberty, according to Proudhon, should be the guiding principle of revolution. However, the pursuit of liberty can destroy liberty because for some people liberty involves the protection from evil and this protection requires control and domination. Proudhon went on to say that revolution should not simply change the colour of tyranny, rather it should lead to the complete destruction of the state. 'To be governed is to be watched over, inspected, spied on, directed, legislated over, regulated, docketed, indoctrinated, preached at, controlled, assessed, weighed, censored, ordered about by men who have neither right, nor knowledge, nor virtue. That is government, that is its justice, that is its morality.' Even though Proudhon was aware that violent revo-

lution carried with it the possibility of an equally tyrannical rule, though with different ends, he saw revolutionary violence as the only way to put an end to state violence.

ANARCHY

Proudhon believed that man was neither good in his natural state nor bad through the material conditions that have created his current nature. For Proudhon, 'Man is by nature a sinner, that is to say not essentially a wrong-doer but rather wrongly made, and his destiny is perpetually to re-create his ideal in himself.' Previous political philosophers, in particular Hobbes, suggested that man's natural nastiness means the only viable form human communities can take is one governed by an absolute state. Proudhon was concerned with expressing his anti-state revolutionary scorn, rather than with producing a workable blueprint for a new society. As a consequence, his ideas about the ideal society were vague. He asked us to imagine a society most would find inconceivable, one where the only function of government, if it is deemed necessary at all, would be nominal. Government, according to Proudhon, should have no real powers and should merely provide a forum for the exchange of views. To realise the ideal society a more enlightened human nature was required. Proudhon argued that this new human nature should contain an overwhelming respect for justice and the needs of others, making the existence of an overbearing state authority unnecessary. However, Proudhon also admitted that this Utopia would not be easily achieved: 'Justice, as we can see from the example of children and savages, is the last and slowest to grow of all the faculties of the soul; it needs an energetic education in struggle and adversity.'

"Man is by nature a sinner, that is to say not essentially a wrongdoer but rather wrongly made, and his destiny is perpetually to re-create his ideal in himself."

WHAT IS TO BE DONE?

Lenin's first significant contribution to political philosophy was a pamphlet entitled *What Is To Be Done?* The title reveals much about Lenin's philosophy. It hints at Lenin's impatience with Marxist theorising, which, he believed, had spent too long discussing the perfect state of revolutionary consciousness among the working classes. Lenin was sceptical that the working classes would generate revolutionary consciousness by themselves at all: 'We said that there could not yet be Social-Democratic consciousness among the workers. This consciousness could only be brought to them from without. The history of all countries shows that the working class, exclusively by its own effort, is able to develop only trade-union consciousness...' Lenin believed that the Revolution had to be brought to the masses by middle-class intellectuals. He believed political consciousness was more than an awareness of exploitation, it was also the ability to organise radical action.

THE REVOLUTIONARY AND THE PRAGMATIST

Lenin knew that for the Bolsheviks to lead Russia to revolution a radical adaptation of Marxist doctrine was needed. According to orthodox Marxism, which argued that revolution and Communism would follow the eras of Feudalism and Capitalism, Feudal Russia in 1917 was not yet ready for revolution. Lenin was not prepared to wait for perfect revolutionary conditions in Russia and his leadership of the Bolshevik Party was based on pragmatism. In keeping with his belief that revolution would be nurtured by middle-class intellectuals, Lenin made the Bolsheviks into a vanguard party – an elite group who preserved

FORCED INTO EXILE IN FINLAND AFTER THE MARCH REVOLUTION, LENIN RETURNED TO LEAD HIS BOLSHEVIK PARTY TO COMMUNIST REVOLUTION IN OCTOBER 1917.

VLADIMIR ILYICH LENIN (1870–1924)

Lenin's contribution to modern philosophy is important principally because he managed to put his ideas into practice. As the leader of the Bolsheviks in the 1917 Russian Revolution, Lenin developed Marxism in a practical context and changed the course of the 20th century.

the true revolutionary values and strategies for their implementation. Lenin thought Marxism was more than an ideology, it was a science. Therefore, the party should be concerned with advancing the science of Marxism and its implementation. Concentrating on this strtegy would bring truth and therefore justice. After the revolution, the party would need to be centrally organised, allowing no autonomy for its constituent parts. Lenin called this form of organisation 'Democratic Centralism'.

THE WAY FORWARD

In his pamphlet *State and Revolution*, which was left unfinished on the eve of the Revolution, Lenin sketched his idea of the type of society the Revolution should create. Lenin suggested that the Marxist dream of the 'withering away' of the state was much further down the revolutionary road than Marxists imagined. He argued that a strong state would be needed for a considerable time in order to enforce proletarian democracy. Lenin called this the 'Dictatorship of the Proletariat'.

TOP LEFT: *THE TSAR, THE PRIEST AND THE RICH MAN* – A COMMUNIST PROPOGANDA POSTER FROM 1918.
ABOVE: AFTER THE REVOLUTION STALIN MANIPULATED THE DIFFERENT WINGS OF THE PARTY TO BECOME LEADER.

LEON TROTSKY (1879–1940)

Leon Trotsky's legacy has been the most enduring of all the intellectual leaders of the Russian Revolution. He played a major part in the Revolution not only through his writing, but also through his public speeches and leadership of the Red Army. Despite his huge commitment to the Bolsheviks, Trotsky retained sufficient intellectual distance from the Revolution for his ideas to be relevant to future revolutionaries. Revolutionary groups across the world have developed strategies and philosophies for revolutionary programmes in his name.

A BORN REVOLUTIONARY

Trotsky was born to comparatively wealthy Jewish farmers in 1879 and was actually named Lev Davidovitch Bronstein, only later acquiring the name Leon Trotsky. By the age of 18, Trotsky had already grasped his destiny as a revolutionary and had helped to form an organisation called the South Russian Workers Union. He soon learnt the dangers of radical politics when he was arrested for his activities and sentenced to four years in Siberia. He was arrested again during the 1905 Revolution and was once more sent to Siberia – though he managed to escape on his journey there.

Trotsky was a key player in the 1917 Revolution, not least because of his peerless skill as a public speaker. A fellow socialist, Sukhanov, spoke of Trotsky's excellent oratory skills when he recalled that Trotsky 'spoke everywhere simultaneously. Every worker and soldier knew him and listened to him. His influence on the masses and the leaders alike was overwhelming.' In the Civil War, which followed the Revolution, Trotsky's leadership of the Red Army was decisive, though often harsh and brutal. When Lenin died in 1922 a struggle for power between Trotsky and Stalin emerged for the leadership of the Communist Party. Trotsky, in retrospect, was ill-suited to the job of leading the country as he was more concerned with the orthodoxy of Marxism than the political expediencies of leadership.

Inevitably, Stalin became leader and Trotsky soon became an 'enemy' of the proletariat. In 1929, after years of trying to convince others of the need for the Revolution to take a different route, Trotsky's opposition was crushed and he was driven into exile. On 20 August 1940, a Russian secret agent named Jacson visited Trotsky's residence in Mexico under the guise of an enthusiastic supporter. As Trotsky read an article that the agent had brought with him Jacson crushed Trotsky's skull with an ice-axe.

PERMANENT REVOLUTION

Trotsky's contribution to revolutionary Marxism is his belief that revolution can only be successful if it is supported by a continual expansion of the proletariat's revolutionary consciousness beyond the country in which revolution initially took place. The spread of revolution beyond Russia would compensate for Russia's inadequacies in terms of industrial progress. This was the theory behind the Comintern organisation set up shortly after the Revolution. Unfortunately, Trotsky's concern for international socialism clashed with Lenin's 'Socialism in One Country' policy. As a result, Trotsky's key theory has never been properly tested.

TROTSKYISM IN THE WEST

For Western Marxists after the Second World War, Trotsky's philosophy had a unique appeal. Through Trotsky Marxists could distance themselves from the atrocities of Stalinism whilst still committing themselves to the virtues of a Communist Utopia.

"It was not the opposition of the liberal bourgeoisie, nor the elemental rising of the peasantry, or the terrorist acts of intelligensia, but the strike of the workers that for the first time brought Tzarism to its knees."

AN ACTIVE MIND

Gramsci's awareness of the political culture of capitalism was initially formed through his participation in the Turin factory strikes between 1916 and 1919. In the aftermath of the First World War, Italy experienced considerable revolutionary fervour, which Gramsci contributed to by providing a theoretical purpose to the social discontent of the Italian working class. His revolutionary ideals were expressed in *L'Ordine Nuovo*, a journal which he and other Marxist intellectuals had founded in 1919. Gramsci's talent for understanding the realities of conflict and political strategy were given a more concrete forum within the Italian Communist Party which he helped to establish in 1921. In 1924, two years after Mussolini's phoney, but successful, coup d'état, Gramsci was elected as a member of the Italian parliament.

ANTONIO GRAMSCI (1891–1937)

The work of the Italian philosopher Antonio Gramsci ranks with the most powerful political and social philosophy written during the 20th century. Gramsci's contribution to modern thinking is all the more impressive given the efforts of the dictator Benito Mussolini to silence him. His incisive and provocative critique of 20th century state capitalism came when the century was barely 30 years old. Yet, many would argue, it is just as relevant now as it was 70 years ago. Even though Gramsci's critique of the Western world has its origins in Marxism its arguments have a poignancy for many who otherwise reject Marxist doctrine.

However, Gramsci's active political career was to be short-lived. In 1926, recognising his threat as an astute and powerful opponent, Mussolini imprisoned him for the remaining 11 years of his life. Nonetheless, it was during this period that Gramsci produced his most important work. Whilst incarcerated and in poor health Gramsci wrote what became known as *The Prison Notebooks*. The notebooks, which in typescript consisted of 4,000 pages, contained a devastating critique of advanced capitalism, updating and surpassing Marx's *Das Capital*.

CAPITALISM

The significance of Gramsci's contribution to Marxist philosophy lies in its recognition of the strength and importance of ruling-class ideology. Marx, and his more orthodox disciples, had previously argued that the ruling classes maintained their power base simply by controlling the means of production, i.e.

industry, upheld through force if necessary. By contrast Gramsci argued that force could only be a short-term measure for the ruling classes, who needed to create popular consent among the working classes to rule effectively and efficiently. That consent was gained by spreading the beliefs of Capitalist ideology through important cultural institutions. Through education, religion, the media, and government bureaucracy the ruling class could create order in civil society by ensuring that basic capitalist values were thought unquestionable.

REVOLUTION

Gramsci, unlike many Marxists, did not believe that revolution would happen spontaneously. The working classes will not suddenly realise an interest in overthrowing the ruling class. 'For a mass of people to be led to think coherently and in the same coherent fashion about the present world, is a "philosophical" event far more important and "original" than the discovery by some philosophical "genius" of a truth which remains the property of a small group of intellectuals.'

Faced with the enormous success of Capitalist ideology the job of the intellectual aiming to effect radical political change is to expose the socio-economic origins of dominant cultural values. However, the intellectual should not remain detached from the culture which he or she is trying to effect: 'A global economic and political policy, if it means to create and secure international socialism, must find a point of contact with trivial, banal, primitive, simple everyday life, with the desires of the broadest masses...'

ABOVE: ANTONIO GRAMSCI'S CONTRIBUTION TO PHILOSOPHY WAS IN BRINGING MARXISM INTO THE TWENTIETH CENTURY. MUSSOLINI SAW GRAMSCI AS A MAJOR THREAT TO HIS FASCIST REGIME. IN 1926 GRAMSCI WAS IMPRISONED. WHILST IN PRISON HE DEVELOPED THE IDEAS WHICH SURPASSED MARX.

COUNTER
ENLIGHTENMENT

By illustrating the darker and uncertain aspects of human experience, the philosophers of the counter enlightenment shattered the triumphant march for reason. This philosophical tradition has benefitted from the literary talents of men such as Hegel, Nietzsche and Sartre.

CHAPTER SEVEN

In 18th and 19th century Europe a new wave of philosophers, poets, writers and artists emerged and became known as the Romantics. Their enormous contribution to European culture and thinking, however, is difficult to pigeon-hole. The poetry of Goethe and Byron, the novels of Rousseau and Shelley and the philosophy of Schopenhauer and Nietzsche do not represent a clear set of ideas which can be shaped into a single movement. The particular aesthetic, literary and philosophical qualities of each of the Romantics, makes categorisation seem a vulgar exercise. Their most common attribute was a questioning of the Enlightenment. However, this attribute also makes them elusive for the historian and philosopher.

THE ROMANTICS

NEBUCHADNEZZAR (BLAKE) - THE ROMANTICS SHOWED MAN IN A NATURAL STATE, QUESTIONING THE ENLIGHTENMENT'S CELEBRATION OF REASON.

In questioning the power and virtue of reason, the Romantics turned their attention to emotion and desire; perennial features of human existence that haunt those who celebrate the rational. In order to study the characteristics of humanity, which were ignored by the Enlightenment, the Romantics turned to aesthetics. Romantic philosophers found that by the aestheticism of their work they created an outlet for the elements of human existence which couldn't be properly expressed through a rationalised, systematic approach. Likewise, Romantic poets and writers channelled their literary skills into a counter-Enlightenment sensibility. Together, the Romantic philosophers and poets created a set of philosophical tensions that continue to inform debates about the meaning of human existence, knowledge, politics and ideas about the good life.

THE AGE OF SENSIBILITY

The Enlightenment view held that the human attribute which most sharply distinguished human beings from animals was reason. Rationality made man separate and therefore progress in human history was born out of its advance. From this foundation, Enlightenment philosophers formulated a set of distinctions between the mind and body and the intellect and senses which were the key to our special status as human beings; the 'senses' and the 'body' were the attributes man shares with animals. The intellect controls the senses, and only when it is in full command of them are truth and justice possible. This is because truth and justice are grounded in rationality.

The Enlightenment had characterised the senses with negative connotations – they were an unruly hindrance to rational progress and to be controlled. Romantic philosophy developed through a reaction to these distinctions and the celebration of rationality. For the Romantic, the intellect can never be separated from the passions of life which embody it. For example, truth and justice cannot be accounted for at the expense of emotion and desire. Passion, beauty and happiness, all aspects of emotion and desire, are integral to any form of human interest.

THE ROMANTIC VIEW OF HUMAN NATURE

Romantic philosophers can often arrive at very different conclusions when speculating about the 'good life'. On the one hand rationality is seen as a threat to human individuality and creativity. Therefore the good life lies in the preservation of the spirit of the individual. Many Romantics maintained a certain nostalgia for man in his natural state. Such nostalgia often resulted in a more optimistic view of human nature than the Enlightenment view of man as naturally savage and egotistic. According to some Romantics, man in his natural state enjoyed a perfect harmony of passion, desire, happiness and peace.

On the other hand the Romantic fetish of aesthetic greatness led to the belief that the good life was achieved by transcending the ordinary banal concerns of the individual. This perspective could lead, paradoxically, to a celebration of the great features of human

GARRICK AND MRS PRITCHARD IN MACBETH BY HENRY FUESLI (1812). THE PASSION, TRAGEDY AND FATALISM THAT CAN BE FOUND IN SHAKESPEARE'S MACBETH ARE CHARACTERISTICS THAT ARE TYPICALLY FOUND IN ROMANTIC LITERATURE.

progress which transcended the individual, for example the State. One of the great originators of European Romanticism, Jean Jacques Rousseau, attempted to represent both of these ideals in one perspective. He believed that the good life was to be found in the realisation of a general will which embodied an absolute incarnation of both ideals. However, Rousseau's Utopian ideal was ultimately unthinkable and unspeakable.

The unthinkable was a common and enduring characteristic of Romantic thinking. This provided a stark contrast with Enlightenment philosophy which was concerned to start, at least, with that which could be known with certainty. The Enlightenment epitomised the values of logic, certainty and consistency and the Romantic revelled in contradiction and uncertainty.

THE ORIGINS OF EXISTENTIALISM

The first philosopher to be labelled an existentialist was the Dane, Soren Kierkegaard. 'In making a choice, it is not so much a question of choosing the right as of the energy, the earnestness, the pathos with which one chooses. Thereby the personality announces its inner infinity, and thereby, in turn, the personality is consolidated.' Kierkegaard's emphasis on the formation of human identity rather than the rational foundations of human existence was a precursor to the later existentialist theories about 'living' and choosing one's existence rather than merely existing. Kierkegaard's own life was a model of existential existence. He once said that if God offered him well-being in the right hand and a life of struggle and eternal striving in the left, he would without hesitation choose the left. In reality, this was not far from the truth, as his own life was filled with solitude and utter melancholy. However, the seeds of existentialism had been sown even before Kierkegaard, both in the anti-rationalism of early Romanticism and in the philosophy of Hegel.

FREE WILL

Existentialist philosophy concentrates upon one's being in the world. It is most concerned with the conditions which we create for our

EXISTENTIALISM

WHILST EXISTENTIALISM IS A PHILOSOPHICAL SCHOOL OF THOUGHT, IT ALSO DENOTES A KIND OF LIFESTYLE. EXCESS AND ECCENTRICITY ARE OFTEN ASSOCIATED WITH THE EXISTENTIALIST.

existence rather than those created by nature. Existentialists tend to judge those conditions by how much they effect human autonomy. That is, to what extent social norms and codes restrict our free will. Measuring the human capacity for free will is extremely difficult. For example, how is it possible to distinguish a decision which is free of all outside influences from one which we take subconsciously because we have internalised the social norms that make us take it?

Existentialists answer this question by arguing that the identity of each individual is his own unique creation. However, this doesn't

1968

The 1968 student revolt in Paris is often seen as a high point of existentialist action. Although the reasons for the revolt and the particular political tensions that created it are removed from Jean-Paul Sartre's discourse on Being and Nothingness, many of the slogans which stoked the students' passion had their origins in the Existentialist movement. The protest was against the inhumane, ordered nature of education in France which restricted individuality.

mean that all human beings share the same level of autonomy. To make full use of one's free will one needs to actively create meaning out of one's existence, rather than allow it to be imposed.

HAPPINESS

Existentialist philosophers are less concerned with happiness than they are with free will. Happiness is not a creative state of mind, according to existentialists. It is akin to a numb state, whereby the individual has become contented with his lot, whereby meaning created by others dictates their life and restricts their free will.

HOLLOW TERM

Existentialism is now a widely recognised movement. But according to the man who is mostly responsible for its promotion, Jean-Paul Sartre, it became too successful: 'the word [Existentialism] is now so loosely applied to so many things that it no longer means anything at all'.

ABOVE: MUCH OF THE PHILOSOPHY BEHIND THE STUDENT RIOTS OF MAY 1968 IN FRANCE ORIGINATED IN EXISTENTIALISM.
LEFT: THE CHIEF ENEMY OF EXISTENTIALISM WAS THE MONOTONY OF MODERN LIFE.

THE DIALECTIC

Hegel's complex philosophical system begins from the idea that the view of the world as made up of separate isolated things or facts is irrational. Only after facts or things are related together into a whole (which Hegel calls the absolute) can one speak of rationality; things-in-themselves are simply impossible. Attempts to posit a thing in its totality inevitably lead to contradiction. The totality of a thing cannot be explained without referring to its relation to something outside it. For example, we cannot completely explain an object such as a hammer without also explaining its functions and, therefore, its relation to other objects.

G.W.F. HEGEL (1770–1831)

Hegel was the most ambitious philosopher the world has ever known. He was born in Stuttgart, the son of a civil servant, and developed his philosophy as a professor at Jena, Nuremberg and Berlin. The task he set himself was to formulate nothing less than a complete explanation of the totality of human experience and existence. No phenomenon is left outside of Hegel's philosophical system. For Hegel 'the truth is the whole'. Despite his concern to explain all phenomena, Hegel was the first thinker to question comprehensively the fundamental basis of Enlightenment thinking.

Furthermore, our knowledge of the object and its relation to other objects is not separate from the object itself. There is no objective world existing outside our attempts, through knowledge, to explain it. The truth is so absolute for Hegel, that it constitutes a singular whole. This means you cannot speak of particular concepts which represent reality. As Hegel says: 'The real is the rational and the rational is the real.' This means that everything real is the generation of concepts (i.e. rationality) and the generation of concepts is the real (reality). This explanation constitutes Hegel's dialectics.

Hegel argues that all the relations, differences and oppositions between concepts are

TOP LEFT: ALTHOUGH DIFFICULT TO UNDERSTAND, HEGEL'S INFLUENCE ON PHILOSOPHY HAS BEEN IMMEASURABLE.
ABOVE: PLATO. HEGEL'S IDEA THAT FREEDOM MEANS ACTING ACCORDING TO UNIVERSALLY VALID PRINCIPLES CAN BE SAID TO HAVE ORIGINATED IN PLATO'S DEPICTION OF THE IDEAL REPUBLIC.

contained in an interrelated unity. There can be no such thing as a self-contained concept. The concept (which he labelled as the thesis) cannot represent reality sufficiently enough because by itself it does not contain its opposite (the antithesis) without which the concept doesn't make sense. Hence we arrive at a synthesis of thesis and antithesis. However, once this synthesis is stated it becomes a thesis in itself and is therefore subject to its own inadequacy as a representation of reality, which in turn produces another antithesis and synthesis and so on. No phenomenon escapes the dialectic: 'Wherever there is movement, wherever there is life, wherever anything is them. In other words, one can only be free by advancing universal rationality, because the more sophisticated our notion of freedom, the more universally valid it becomes. Hegel celebrated everything that represented universal rationality, in particular the State. For Hegel, the State is the absolute incarnation of rationality as it represents the point of synthesis of all differences and conflicts in society through its governing: 'The essence of the state is the universal, self-originated, and self-developed-the reasonable spirit of the will; but, as self-knowing and self-actualising, sheer subjectivity, and as an actuality-one individual.'

carried into effect in the actual world, the Dialectic is at work.'

THE STATE AND FREEDOM

Hegel thought there is a spirit which drives the dialectic. This spirit is the dialectic of history which encompasses everything. No event in history stands alone as a single identifiable moment. The logic of the dialectic is obviously rationality, but the spirit of rationality is freedom. Hegel's idea of freedom is not one which most of us would recognise. For Hegel, freedom doesn't mean the freedom to do as one wishes, it means acting according to universally valid principles and thus advancing

PAUL GAUGUIN'S PAINTING *WHERE DO WE COME FROM? WHAT ARE WE? WHERE ARE WE GOING?* REPRESENTS THE AMBITIOUS NATURE OF HEGEL'S PHILOSOPHY, THE SCOPE OF WHICH WAS LITTLE SHORT OF AN ABSOLUTE UNDERSTANDING OF HUMAN EXPERIENCE.

ARTHUR SCHOPENHAUER (1788–1860)

Arthur Schopenhauer.

Schopenhauer is one of the few philosophers, like Nietzsche and Rousseau, whose philosophy contains literary power as well as philosophical insight. He is classified as a Romantic philosopher for this reason and because he was angered by the atomistic and technical philosophy of the Enlightenment. Schopenhauer was born to wealthy Dutch traders in Danzig, Germany, in 1788. But he rejected his parents' hope that he would take over the family business and, instead, followed his intellectual instincts. His taste for philosophy, however, was not acquired until after he had completed a Degree in Medicine at Gottingen University in 1811. He quickly made up for lost time, though, and seven years into his philosophical career he had completed his two-volume book which, remarkably, expressed views from which he never deviated.

SCHOPENHAUER BELIEVED THAT HIS UNSURPASSED MASTERY OF IMMANUEL KANT, THE GREATEST OF ALL GERMAN PHILOSOPHERS, WOULD MAKE HIM THE MOST FAMOUS LIVING PHILOSOPHER IN EUROPE.

FAME AND KANT

Schopenhauer was certain that his book *The World as Will and Idea* would make him the most famous living philosopher in Europe. But unfortunately the only fame that he received was posthumous. Schopenhauer believed that his fame was assured because he alone had understood the greatest of all German philosophers, Immanuel Kant. The identity of 19th century German philosophy was almost wholly defined by its relation to Kant. To produce the most perfect understanding of Kant and to construct a philosophy therein was tantamount to solving the problem of philosophy.

The critical aspect of Kant's philosophy was his view on the origins and construction of knowledge. Kant was famously awoken from his intellectual slumbers by reading the Scottish philosopher Hume's arguments that human knowledge had no more foundation than experience. This meant that the human perception of truth is not grounded in any permanent attributes of the human mind. Kant knew that Hume was wrong about this but found it difficult to prove him wrong. He knew that, whilst it was difficult to prove, the human appreciation of the truth of 2+2=4 was unshakeable, and whilst not entirely innate, by no means as contingent as Hume had assumed.

THE WILL

Schopenhauer's aim was to further Kant's view of human knowledge. One might assume, therefore, that Schopenhauer's philosophy would be equally as difficult and systematic as the austere and jargon-filled philosophy of Kant. Actually, much of Schopen-hauer's writing is lucid, clear and at the same time romantic: 'The true philosopher will indeed always seek after light and perspicuity, and will strive to resemble a Swiss lake – which through its calm is enabled to unite great depth with great clearness, the depth revealing itself precisely by reason of the clearness – rather than a turbid, impetuous mountain torrent.' Like many of his Romantic contemporaries, Schopenhauer's aim was to

arrive at truths by tapping into a literary sensibility which expressed human understanding, rather than creating a systematic logic. The 'well of human understanding' that Schopenhauer believed he was expressing and writing about was what he called the human will or 'the will'. For Schopenhauer, 'it was that which exists independently of our perception, that which actually is. To Democritus it was matter; fundamentally this was what it still was to Locke; to Kant it was = x; to me it is will.' It is difficult to summarise precisely what Schopenhauer meant by this, because despite the clarity of his philosophy, nearly all his work is an explanation of 'the will'. In essence he argued that all human actions and knowledge are constituted by the human will. 'It is only in reflection that to will and to act are different; in reality they are one.' This all-encompassing human will is characterised by Schopenhauer as a blind striving power which 'reveals itself to everyone directly as the in-itself of his own phenomenal being'.

SCHOPENHAUER REJECTED CHRISTIANITY IN FAVOUR OF BUDDHISM AND HINDUISM. THESE RELIGIONS HAD A GREAT INFLUENCE ON HIS PHILOSOPHY.

PRUSSIAN PRODIGY

Nietzsche was born the son of a Protestant pastor on 15 October 1844, in Rochen, Prussia. By the age of 25, and before he had even completed his doctorate, Nietzsche's brilliance was rewarded with the status of Professor of classical philosophy at the University of Basel. At around this time, Nietzsche befriended the German composer Wagner. The two men greatly admired one another, but they quarrelled frequently.

In 1872, Nietzsche's first book, *The Birth of Tragedy*, was published and in 1878 his seminal work, the celebrated *Human all too Human*, went into print. But the remainder of Nietzsche's career was hampered by his failing health. In 1879 he was forced to resign from his chair at Basel as his physical condition had deteriorated. For the next ten years he led a solitary existence, wandering from hotel rooms and lodgings. He never married and his fear and contempt of women was reflected in his writing.

But despite his nomadic lifestyle, Nietzsche produced some of his most important works during this period. *Thus Spoke Zarathustra* (1883), *Beyond Good and Evil* (1886), *On the Genealogy of Morality* (1887), *The Anti-Christ* (1888), *Ecce Homo* (1888) and *The Twilight of the Idols* (1889) were all written as Nietzsche wandered his way through Europe.

NIETZSCHE'S POSTHUMOUS NOTORIETY

In 1889 Nietzsche's mental health began to deteriorate and on 25 August 1890 he died alone and insane. Nietzsche had proclaimed that his writing was for the future and that it would not be understood by his contemporaries. This assertion proved correct as interest in his work has grown throughout the 20th century, particularly in France and America.

TRUTH AND SCEPTICISM

Many commentators have condemned Nietzsche's ethics while praising his philosophical insight, but the two qualities cannot be separated without diluting his philosophy. The key to Nietzsche's thinking is his philosophical scepticism. He believed that truth is merely a cultural necessity. That is, that there is no fundamental truth that lies beneath language and which exists in the nature of things. There is no moral truth and no scientific natural truth that governs our existence. For Nietzsche, references to truth are governed by the cultural need to bracket, segment and

FRIEDRICH NIETZSCHE (1844–90)

Nietzsche is the most notorious philosopher the world has known. Like many great thinkers, his work is both admired and condemned in equal measure. He was a cultural aristocrat who despised what he saw as the growing decadence of European culture in the 19th century. He blamed this moral decline on the prevalence of democratic ideas, Christian values and the 'impurity' of the dominant European races. Such thinking was later praised by Adolf Hitler in *Mein Kampf*. This unfortunate legacy has greatly contributed to Nietzsche's fame – although the quality of his work should not be underestimated.

control our experience of the world. According to Nietzsche, truth is nothing more than an expedient condition of language.

If there is no moral truth then there can be no absolute notions of good and evil. Nietzsche said that it is a mistake to strive for the victory of good and the annihilation of evil. This quest is central to Christianity, but for Nietzsche Christianity only produced what he described as 'slave morality'. He felt that Christianity tamed the heart in man and must be condemned for denying the value of 'exuberant spirits, splendid animalism, the instincts of war and conquest, the deification of passion, revenge, anger, voluptuousness, adventure, knowledge'. For Nietzsche, if one cannot speak of good and evil then one is left to measure the value of things and people in terms of greatness and excellence. The measure of greatness is the power of 'the will'. That is, the power to overcome others' morality and others' suffering in the pursuit of great art and strong leadership.

GOD IS DEAD

Nietzsche prophesied a great deal, and in *Thus Spoke Zarathustra* he famously proclaimed that 'God is dead'. He meant that the slave morality of European culture would die away and that the understanding of good and evil would crumble into uncertainty. This prophecy has been more accurate than some of the Marxist predictions. His incisive commentary on Western culture and his

BORN IN THE MID-19TH CENTURY, NIETZSCHE'S COUNTER-ENLIGHTENMENT THINKING HAS STRUCK A CHORD WITH MANY MODERN MINDS. NIETZSCHE BELIEVED THAT THE WORLD WAS MAN-MADE AND THAT GREATNESS AND EXCELLENCE – RATHER THAN GOOD AND EVIL – SHOULD BE USED TO MEASURE VALUE. STRONG LEADERSHIP WAS ESSENTIAL. UNSURPRISINGLY, HITLER REINTERPRETED NIETZSCHE'S WORK TO SUPPORT HIS FASCIST PHILOSOPHY.

powerful anti-Enlightenment thinking have ensured that Nietzsche's popularity has grown since his premature death.

NIETZSCHE'S LEGACY

The impact of Nietzsche's work on 20th century philosophy has been enormous. Only Marx and Freud have had a greater impact on 20th century thinking. Nietzsche questioned the old certainties of Western thought – a tradition that has been taken forward by the powerful philosophical movements of the 20th century.

Nietzsche's influence is evident in the existentialist philosophy of Martin Heidegger and Jean-Paul Sartre, and more significantly the postmodern philosophy of the 1990s. Postmodernism has furthered Nietzsche's destructive insights into the dominant values of human existence. Nietzsche's thinking has also made significant contributions to many aspects of modern culture that are outside of the academic arena.

self-importance was not recognised by the Nazi Party, who needed a Nazi-supporting bureaucrat to implement changes in all universities rather than a spiritual leader. Frustrated by his lack of recognition Heidegger resigned as rector in April 1934.

BEING AND TIME

In his most important work, *Being and Time*, Heidegger poses the question: *what is being?* He sets out to dismantle the idea, dominant in the West since Plato, that human beings have an essence, and that the world is made up of

MARTIN HEIDEGGER (1889-1976)

Heidegger is the most enigmatic philosopher of the 20th century. His philosophy is notoriously complex and somewhat mysterious. It is difficult not because of any philosophical pretensions, but because the task Heidegger set himself was enormous. It entails nothing less than the ripping away of the foundations of Western thought; foundations Heidegger believes were established by Plato, solidified in the Enlightenment and so ingrained in our understanding of the world that they are unquestioned by all but the most sceptical and inquisitive.

Born in Messkirch, Germany, in 1889, Heidegger's initial ambitions were in theology. However, his attempts to become a priest, a theology student and a professor of Catholic theology all failed. This was in part due to ill-health, but also because of the judgements of academics who thought him unsuitable. This rejection fuelled Heidegger's ambition and generated a certain resentment in his character. In April 1933 Heidegger was elected Rector of Freiburg University. Soon after that, he joined the Nazi Party. He believed that his position and intellectual supremacy would make him the intellectual and spiritual leader of Nazism in Germany. However, Heidegger's

entities, which can be categorised, reduced and calculated. Most philosophers had previously assumed that the world was made up of certain entities and had merely attempted to locate them and identify their relationships with one another. For Heidegger, however, those philosophers neglected to examine the conditions that enable us to identify and understand the world. These conditions are essentially made up by language and culture, but they also include the everyday values, attitudes and feelings that make up human existence, i.e. our moods and anxieties. An examination of such conditions reveals that it is the values and contingencies involved in the process of understanding entities rather than the entities themselves which determine the meanings we attach to the world. Those entities we identify as real in particular ways are nothing more than meanings.

> SOME ACADEMICS HAVE ARGUED THAT YOU CANNOT UNDERSTAND THE INTELLECTUAL COMPOSITION OF THE 20TH CENTURY WITHOUT UNDERSTANDING HEIDEGGER'S PHILOSOPHY.

THE NATURE OF LANGUAGE

Heidegger believed that when we are born we are thrown into a world with pre-established norms and standards which include the tools we use to describe ourselves and our relation to the world. We are not born innately with the instruments of rationality. But Heidegger is presenting much more than a simple nurture over nature argument. For Heidegger, language is not just a medium through which we express our imperfect views of the world, it *is* the world. To believe otherwise is to believe that somehow nature and truth have a language which was somehow bestowed upon us rather than invented.

For Heidegger, a consideration of the way we understand the world will shatter our assumed certainties. We cannot describe the world without recourse to metaphor and storytelling. When we give meanings we inevitable do so in certain contexts otherwise they are meaningless.

HEIDEGGER AND THE NAZIS

As well as joining the Nazi Party Heidegger tried to give Nazism philosophical support. He suggested that Nazi Germany could bring to the world a new beginning comparable to that initiated by Ancient Greece. Philosophers continue to speculate about whether his work

has an in-built inclination to Nazism. This is, in part, because after reading Heidegger one could be tempted to believe that all political institutions of democracy and justice established by the Enlightenment and the political theory of the 18th and 19th centuries have no rational foundation which ought to command our respect.

NAUSEA

The best way to understand Sartre's philosophy is through his novels and plays. His most deeply philosophical novel is *Nausea*. The central character of the book, Antoine Roquentin, is portrayed as a man whose comfortable rationalism is inexplicably overcome by an overpowering sense of uncertainty about reality and his place within it. As he picks up a stone or looks at his face in the mirror he wonders what it means for things to exist and, most frighteningly, what makes up his own existence, its past, present and future. Roquentin describes his anguish: 'It took my breath … At one blow it was there … The diversity of things, their individuality, was nothing but an appearance, a varnish. This varnish had melted. What was left were monstrous soft masses in disorder, naked in frightening nudity.' He realises that there is no pattern to the events of his life – the past can be remembered only in fragments and he is not sure of its reality. Perhaps only the present can be real, but what is the present? The present never actually happens, it is just an 'I' which he cannot define. This uncertainty about the world is a familiar philosophical

JEAN PAUL-SARTRE (1905–80)

Jean Paul-Sartre is just as famous as Plato, Aristotle or Kant. In post-war France he achieved cult status and when he died in 1980, Parisians attended his funeral in unprecedented numbers. There is good reason for Sartre's fame. Even though Sartre's philosophy contains much philosophical jargon, his ideas can be translated into values which can be appropriated for everyday life. He provided a philosophy which every individual could act upon and offered a practical explanation of the world rather than one merely concerned with its internal coherence.

TOP LEFT: JEAN-PAUL SARTRE WAS AMONG THE MOST ENIGMATIC FIGURES OF EUROPEAN PHILOSOPHY IN THE 20TH CENTURY.
ABOVE: PARISIAN CAFÉ SOCIETY IN THE 1930s CAPTURED THE SPIRIT OF SARTRE'S EXISTENTIALISM.

tactic used as a prelude to the discovery of the light of existence or truth. In *Meditations*, Descartes's philosophical revelations are preceded by an all-encompassing doubt which he feels duty bound to answer. However, Roquentin's doubt is answered in a different way to that of Descartes. He does not arrive at a philosophical system of thought which allows him to understand what is and is not real. Instead, the doubt is overcome rather than answered. Roquentin realises, after listening to some beautifully crafted music, that he can overcome the anguish of doubt by creating something of his own which enables him to look back on his life with the feeling that his past has been a progression towards his own creation of the present. He decides to give meaning to his life by writing a novel.

BEING AND NOTHINGNESS

Sartre's most important contribution to philosophy is *Being and Nothingness*, in which he attempts to tackle the question of existence. His philosophy begins by suggesting that all of us have an unavoidable sense of the brute factuality of existence. This sense is vague and indefinite but it is also unshakeable.

Sartre calls this state Being-in-itself. One can be overcome by this vagueness but essentially the indefiniteness of the sense of existence we all have means each individual is his, or her, own world.

BAD FAITH AND FREEDOM

Sartre argued that there are as many worlds as individuals, and countered the argument that the meaning of existence is determined by an objective natural world by asserting that the world would have no meaning if human beings did not act, choose and make decisions which give the world meaning. For Sartre, freedom entails the realisation of this state of affairs. It should 'reveal to the moral agent that he is the being by whom values come into existence. It is then that his freedom will become conscious of itself and will reveal itself in anguish as the unique source of value and the nothingness through which the world exists'. There arises a potential contradiction in Sartre's philosophy here, because if each individual constitutes his own world then how can an individual fail to pursue an authentic existence which he arrives at via a purely conscious decision?

ABOVE: SARTRE USED BOTH THEATRE AND NOVELS AS VEHICLES FOR HIS EXISTENTIAL BELIEFS. THIS 1952 PRODUCTION OF *THE FLIES* HAS A TYPICALLY BLEAK SET.
LEFT: SARTRE'S LOVER SIMONE DE BEAUVOIR MADE AN EQUALLY SIGNIFICANT CONTRIBUTION TO THE PHILOSOPHY OF EXISTENTIALISM. HOWEVER, THE TRIALS OF THEIR RELATIONSHIP GENERATED AS MUCH SPECULATION AS THEIR PHILOSOPHY.

SCIENCE
AND
UTILITY

Philosophy is widely regarded as a purely academic discipline; with neither practical implications nor a basis in tangible evidence. However, in the 19th century a branch of philosophy emerged which was to place emphasis on empirical research and useful application.

CHAPTER EIGHT

THE VIENNA CIRCLE

The Vienna school were a group of philosophers, scientists and mathematicians who met during the 1920s and 30s to discuss the foundations of science and philosophy. The circle was established by Moritz Schlick, a Professor of Philosophy at the University of Vienna. The most distinguished members of the circle included Rudolf Carnap, Herbert Feigl, Kurt Godel, Otto Neurath and Friedrich Waismann. Their intentions were clear. They wanted to rid philosophy completely of what they saw as meaningless metaphysics. To extinguish totally from philosophy the idea that one could credibly produce unprovable truths about human existence which tran-

VIENNA AND OXBRIDGE

scended science. Typical of such truths were those held by the philosopher who was credited with establishing the foundations of Western philosophy, Plato. For it was Plato who had initially speculated that there existed certain universal forms and ideas which the philosopher had privileged access to. The search for those ideas took up a great deal of Western philosophy thereafter – a search which the members of the Vienna Circle believed to be utterly meaningless. Because of these beliefs the Vienna school quickly developed a reputation for the ruthless rubbishing of what they saw as idle and ungrounded philosophical speculation. Once the meaninglessness of metaphysics has been established,

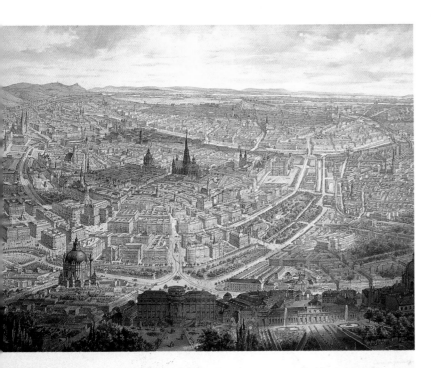

RIGOR IN ARGUMENT EPITOMISED THE STYLE OF THE PHILOSOPHY AMONG OXFORD AND CAMBRIDGE PHILOSOPHY DONS, WHO TRIED TO BRING PHILOSOPHY CLOSER TO NATURAL SCIENCE THROUGH 'ANALYTIC PHILOSOPHY'.

the job of philosophy changes to that of establishing what is and what is not nonsense. In other words, to establish a set of criteria which could be used to ascertain the truthfulness of statements and propositions.

THE OXBRIDGE PHILOSOPHERS

The philosophers sometimes referred to as the Oxbridge philosophers did not make up a school in the same style as the Vienna school. If one philosophical category were to be used to group together the Oxbridge philosophers it would be analytic philosophy. Analytic philosophers tend, though not exclusively, to be English-speaking academics from the mid-19th century onwards. Analytic philosophy, as practised by its primary exponents Bertrand Russell and Ludwig Wittgenstein, is mainly concerned with concepts and propositions. In their eyes, while it did not exhaust the domain of philosophy, analysis provided a vital tool for laying bare the logical form of reality. According to Wittgenstein, who was the heir of Bertrand Russell at Cambridge University in the early part of this century, the structure of language reveals the structure of the world; every meaningful sentence is analysable into atomic constituents of reality.

After Wittgenstein, analytic philosophy at Oxford and Cambridge came to be dominated by what was called Ordinary Language Philosophy. Philosophers of this persuasion focused on the role of words in the lives of ordinary speakers, hoping thereby to escape some long-standing philosophical muddles. These muddles were created by what they thought to be a natural tendency, when pursuing philosophical theses, to be misled by the grammatical form of sentences in which philosophical questions were posed. One example of such a muddle is the philosopher Martin Heidegger's supposition that 'nothing' must designate something, though a very peculiar something. There is very much a scientific feel to analytic philosophy, especially with regard to the way in which the results of their philosophy are disseminated, the practice being to address one another rather than the outside world.

JEREMY BENTHAM
(1748-1832)

The Enlightenment did much to transform views about science, religion and the role of governments, but its achievements in terms of social organisation were less impressive. Religious ideas about the ordering of society were inevitably diluted by secular thinking about the authority of states which stemmed from the Enlightenment. A value system was urgently needed to replace or complement that of the old order. The English philosopher Jeremy Bentham was one of the philosophers who worked to develop a new value system to replace religion.

However, Bentham is more than just a philosopher, he was an architect of the society which led to modern Western Europe. In particular, his ethics and views on law provided much of the social basis for liberal democracy.

LEGAL BACKGROUND

Bentham was born in 1748, the son of a London attorney. He went to Oxford to study at a much younger age than his contemporaries and began his adult life in the legal profession. But Bentham soon became tired of what he saw as the irrational basis of the law in England. He regarded English law as ad hoc and arbitrary. He hoped that the principles which guided the law could take their inspiration from the sciences rather than unadulterated privilege, self-interest and superstition which guided them in the 18th century. With the aid of an allowance from his father, Bentham began studying and writing about the law. By his own admittance, Bentham's work made little impact until the beginning of the 19th century when he applied himself to specific, practical matters of social policy and government.

BENTHAM'S REVOLUTIONARY DESIGN OF THE PERFECT PRISON – THE PANOPTICON – WAS INITIALLY REJECTED BY THE BRITISH GOVERNMENT.

THE GREATEST HAPPINESS PRINCIPLE

In his most celebrated book, *An Introduction to the Principles of Morals and Legislation*, Bentham outlined the basis of his philosophy. He wrote: 'Nature has placed mankind under the governance of two sovereign masters, pain and pleasure. It is for them to point out what we ought to do, as well as to determine what we shall do. On the one hand the standard of right and wrong, on the other the chain of causes and effects, are fastened to their throne.' Later, in *The Rationale of Judicial Evidence*, he wrote: 'In morals, as in legislation, the principle of utility is that which holds up to view as the only sources and tests of right and wrong, human suffering and enjoyment, pain and pleasure.' Taken together these two statements hold the key to Bentham's philosophy. The basis of Bentham's philosophy is an extremely simple formula. Pleasure is good and pain is bad. Governments should, therefore, observe the following principle: '...the greatest number of them, on every occasion on which the nature of the case renders the provision of an equal quantity of happiness for every one of them impossible, by its being a matter of necessity, to make sacrifice of a portion of the happiness of a few, to the greater happiness of the rest.' Therefore decisions should be made to ensure that pleasure outweighs pain. The real radicalism of Bentham's approach was, however, the way in which he applied this principle to social and political issues.

BENTHAM'S THEORY OF PUNISHMENT

Penology formed a major part of Bentham's applied work. There was little doubt that his background in the legal profession helped him to develop his ideas in this direction. The key to Bentham's theory of punishment was the *Hedonistic Calculus*, which was an adapted form of the greatest value principle. According to Bentham, the degree of punishment should be proportional to the level of wrongdoing. However, the degree of punishment should be such that the level of pain inflicted for criminality outweighed the benefits gained from illegal activity.

TOP: THE CAMPAIGN FOR UNIVERSAL SUFFRAGE: BENTHAM WAS REMARKABLE FOR THE WAY IN WHICH HE APPLIED SOCIAL AND POLITICAL PHILOSOPHY TO PRACTICAL ISSUES.
ABOVE: GEORGE III. BENTHAM USED THE MONARCHY OF THE TIME AS A MODEL FOR HIS MORAL PHILOSOPHY.

The philosophic tradition established by René Descartes in the 17th century progressed to its most extreme in the analytical philosophy of Bertrand Russell. The first significant exponent of analytical philosophy was the German philosopher Gottlob Frege (1848–1925). His work begins with a rejection of attempts, by previous philosophers, to ground truth in human knowledge upon speculation about the natural or psychological make-up of humanity. The analytical view reduced philosophy to the apparently less speculative realm of objective logical inquiry. In the philosophy of Bertrand Russell, philosophical certainty, as opposed to philosophical idealism or Utopianism, reaches a purity that few have matched. However, Russell's voluminous philosophical output also included social and political philosophy, which was largely responsible for his widespread fame.

BERTRAND RUSSELL
(1872–1970)

A MATHEMATICIAN AND PHILOSOPHER

Russell was dedicated to his work and he wrote over 40 books, but his public life was, nonetheless, eventful. Born the son of the first Earl Russell, Bertrand's education followed the traditional path of the English upper classes and he eventually found himself studying mathematics at Trinity College, Cambridge, in 1890. After obtaining a fellowship from Cambridge, Russell travelled to America and Germany, where he wrote his first book, which was on German social democracy. His first serious philosophical work entitled *The Principles of Mathematics*, however, was not published until 1903.

Russell's interest in philosophy was ignited by his disillusionment with mathematics. He found the teaching of mathematics to be limited by its insufficient concern with the philosophical foundations of mathematical truths. Nonetheless, the spirit of the mathematician was never to leave him and he pursued his philosophy with an unrelenting rigour. His aim was to purify philosophy by eliminating its speculative content and allowing only pure unmediated fact to serve as its foundation. Those facts, Russell believed, were constituted by a world made up of independent elements. However, not all of the elements regarded as independent are true entities. Some elements are logical fictions because they have meanings which are essentially derived from other more simple elements. In other words, all truth can be reduced to a series of logically independent facts, which have a logical coherence.

*Daddy, what did **YOU** do in the Great War?*

WITTGENSTEIN AND LENIN

The most important event in Russell's life was his relationship with the brilliant young philosopher Ludwig Wittgenstein who arrived at Cambridge in 1912. Russell never fully recovered from Wittgenstein's comprehensive destruction of the idea that a pure philosophical theory of knowledge was possible.

During the First World War Russell was imprisoned for his pacifism. In 1920 he travelled to the newly formed Soviet Republic expecting to find an alternative to what he saw as destructive capitalism. His expectations were dis-appointed however, by the 'unspeakably horrible' regime led by Lenin. Despite his rejection of Leninist Communism which he elaborated upon in his book *The Practice and Theory of Bolshevism*, Russell became one of Britain's principal advocates of radical reform. The clarity and rigour evident in his philosophical work were put to use in journalism and the writing of political pamphlets which brought complex political ideas to a wider public.

PHILOSOPHER AND EDUCATIONALIST

John Dewey was born in Vermont, in 1859, and studied at the state university. After graduating he attended the John Hopkins graduate school and his first teaching post was at a high school in Oil City. Dewey eventually became a professor of philosophy at Chicago, but he is equally famous for his achievements as an educationalist. His advocation of a more progressive approach to education had a significant impact on America. His suggestion that learning by rote needed to be replaced by a way of teaching which engaged the pupil more actively in the subject matter met with a great deal of criticism at the time, but today Dewey's work is pivotal in all theories of education. Dewey was also a passionate Democrat, which is reflected in his sizeable literary output. His political passions took him to China and Japan but his most famous political adventure was in Mexico, where he chaired an inquiry into whether Leon Trotsky should be deported to the USSR for trial by Joseph Stalin.

PRAGMATISM

In *The Quest for Certainty* Dewey argues that the traditional philosophical quest to discover permanent truths based on certain, unchanging knowledge of the world is a futile activity. For Dewey, the world which philosophy hoped to capture in certain knowledge is a permanently changing one. The criterion of truth is not given by permanent structures of reality, it is given by experience. For this reason philosophy rarely makes a difference in practice because it tries to find an Archimedean point of objectivity beyond experience and thus practice.

However, philosophers could respond to this by suggesting that pure philosophy need not be concerned at all with making a difference to practice. It can simply continue to search for the truth regardless of this. Dewey

John Dewey was the foremost exponent of Pragmatism, the most distinctive philosophical school to emerge from America. The fact that this school was born in America is significant, because before Pragmatism Western philosophy was a European affair. It was in Europe that the contours of philosophical thought were etched around the work of Kant and Hegel. Pragmatism was developed by the American philosopher William James (1842–1910) and embodied distinctively American values. Before Pragmatism, these values seemed incompatible with Western philosophy. The anti-intellectualism of American culture which shunned the cultural elitism associated with European philosophy had no philosophical outlet. In Pragmatism it found one. This is why European intellectuals reacted negatively, and indeed many still do, to the Pragmatists' attempt to bring philosophy down to earth.

JOHN DEWEY
(1859–1952)

FRANCIS X. KING

133.4

1987

HAMLYN

answered this by further questioning that search. He asked: 'Can we expect there to be a quality present in all specific verifications, which "truth", noun singular and absolute, can summarise?' The short answer to this question for Dewey is no. According to Dewey 'Truth is a collection of truths.' Truth is simply what statements we agree to characterise with the word true.

Dewey wanted to alter the role that philosophy had prescribed for itself. He wanted to change it from a discipline which attempts to arbitrate in different claims to truth in the outside world, to a discipline which actually tries to advance our well-being.

The best indication of Dewey's pragmatism was his application of it to social and political issues. For Dewey, instead of trying to base our political imagination on what we believe to be more truthful accounts of human nature and human needs, we should base it on what ideas offer the best possibility of widespread

agreement. The best political system must be one which provides the conditions for widespread agreement about the way forward. In this respect democracy was far superior to any other proposed system. However, agreement about the way forward can only be valid if all those who are affected by such an agreement can participate equally in its establishment. Dewey believed passionately that liberal democracy, whilst being the best political system available, was a long way short of offering equal participation.

ABOVE: DEWEY WAS A PASSIONATE COMMENTATOR ON SOCIAL AND POLITICAL ISSUES. HE BELIEVED THAT THE PRINCIPLES WHICH FOUNDED AMERICAN DEMOCRACY WERE BOTH THE BASIS OF FURTHERING DEMOCRACY AND PARADOXICALLY A THREAT TO DEMOCRACY.
DEWEY IS AS FAMOUS FOR HIS WORK ON EDUCATION AS HE IS FOR PHILOSOPHY. IN AMERICA DEWEY'S WORK HAD A CONSIDERABLE IMPACT ON EDUCATION AND LED TO A MORE PROGRESSIVE STYLE OF TEACHING. HE WAS ALSO RESPONSIBLE FOR THE INNOVATIVE DEWEY DECIMAL SYSTEM OF LIBRARY CATALOGING (FAR LEFT).

KARL POPPER (1902–95)

One of philosophy's most persistent themes since the 18th century has been its attempt to explain the success of science. This is because the progress of science has not only dominated Western civilisation, but also threatened the relevance and value of philosophy. Why should academics pursue philosophy if science can provide answers to the meaning of existence with more vigour and certainty? At the turn of the 20th century more philosophers were willing to concede to the supremacy of science on matters which philosophy had previously claimed privileged knowledge of. Indeed, a growing number were transferring scientific ideas and practices to philosophy. Karl Popper's contribution to philosophy lies in providing one of the most powerful accounts of scientific progress. He achieved this chiefly by providing a theory of how science works and how it can be distinguished from non-science.

Popper was born in Vienna in 1902. As a young student he became actively involved in Marxist politics in an increasingly charged political atmosphere in Vienna in the 1930s. With his family's Jewish background in mind Popper had the foresight to leave Vienna and from 1937 to 1945 he taught philosophy at the University of New Zealand. After the war he came to England and in 1949 became Professor of Logic and Scientific Method at the London School of Economics. Popper was knighted in 1965. He lived in England until he died in 1995.

SCIENTIFIC METHOD

When Popper wrote *The Logic of Scientific Discovery Tractatus* (Logik der Foeschung), and to a lesser extent today, the standard view of scientific method and its distinctiveness was dominated by the theory of induction. According to this view science proceeds by first collecting facts gathered from objective observation. Once the facts have been collected they are examined for patterns and connections which may suggest a certain hypothesis about a certain phenomenon. For example, water boils at 100 degrees. The hypothesis is then tested via experiments and then proven to be true or false. Popper vigorously rejected the theory of induction. He argued that science proceeds in precisely the reverse direction. Scientists begin with the premise of a theory and then they accumulate facts. According to Popper, there are no raw, neutral facts or observations which are not presupposed by a theory. One simply cannot observe a fact without at first having some theoretical notion of its significance. Facts do not simply make themselves aware to us. It is more the case that scientists first proceed by making bold theories which explain certain phenomena and then strenuously test those theories until they are replaced by new ones. Popper calls this process falsification. The logical consequence of Popper's theory of falsification is that no theory can ever be true. This is because no theory can ever be closed to scrutiny and therefore falsification.

THE OPEN SOCIETY AND ITS ENEMIES

Popper also applied his theory to social and political philosophy. He argued that any such philosophy which claimed to be closed to vigorous interrogation was denying its own status as a theory. According to Popper, even though Marxism contributed significantly to the falsification of much social theory it cannot uphold its claim to be scientific. This is because Marxism is essentially irrefutable. It has in-built self-defence mechanisms which enable it to explain all phenomena without upsetting its theoretical coherence.

PLATO'S PHILOSOPHY EPITOMISED EVERYTHING THAT POPPER BELIEVED WAS THE ENEMY OF THE OPEN SOCIETY.

141

The common assumption is that through Thales and Pythagoras, Galileo and Newton and then Einstein, science has moved progressively closer to truth. Kuhn's philosophy, which has attracted a great deal of controversy, challenges this view and offers a different view of science. Kuhn fundamentally questions the authority of science and its practices.

THOMAS KUHN (1922–)

THROUGH HIS PHILOSOPHY OF PARADIGMS, KUHN ARGUED THAT ONE COULD NOT TELL WHETHER GALILEO (ABOVE) WAS ANY CLOSER TO SCIENTIFIC TRUTH THAN CONTEMPORARY SCIENTISTS ARE.

PHYSICIST AND PHILOSOPHER

Kuhn was born in Cincinnati, Ohio, in 1922 the son of a German-Jewish family who had emigrated to America during the 19th century. His father came from a banking family, but had trained as an engineer and worked as an industrial consultant; his mother came from a family of New York lawyers. Neither of his parents were strict Jews and Kuhn himself has been true to their secular instincts. The example set by his parents was important to his intellectual development. From his would-be engineer father he inherited an interest in science and from his mother a taste for the arts. Kuhn incorporated both interests into his own preoccupation with the history and philosophy of science. To cement his interest in science Khun went to Harvard in 1940 and majored in physics. After working as a scientist for the US war effort Kuhn decided that life as a physicist wasn't for him and he pursued his interest in the history and philosophy of science instead. This culminated in his now classic work *The Structure of Scientific Revolutions*, which was published in 1962.

CHALLENGE TO SCIENCE

The Structure of Scientific Revolutions contained an uncompromising and unsettling message for scientists. It suggested that their view of scientific development, as a heroic linear process, was a mythic delusion. He argued that a detailed examination of the history of science reveals a very different picture. By challenging the scientific community Kuhn also challenged the Anglo-American philosophical community which had tried hard to justify the received view of scientific development.

Kuhn's alternative to the scientific community's view of its own history was simple and, at first glance, unthreatening. He argued that scientific development was divided into two apparent phases:

1. Long periods of 'normal science' where step-by-step advancements were made within a 'paradigm' (the dominant framework of a set of ideas).

2. Shorter periods of revolutionary change when a 'paradigm' has decayed and rivals were fighting to take its place. A good example of this is the period after Newton published his work on gravity and light. After some scepticism scientists accepted Newton's views as true and used them as a conclusive theory for scientific research for a considerable period; that is until Einstein.

Kuhn also suggested that the legitimacy of a particular paradigm was decided by its acceptability to the prevailing scientific community rather than by reference to objective scientific norms. He thereafter suggested that 'paradigms' were to a large degree self-justifying and so untranslatable, or in Kuhn's terms 'incommensurable' to one another.

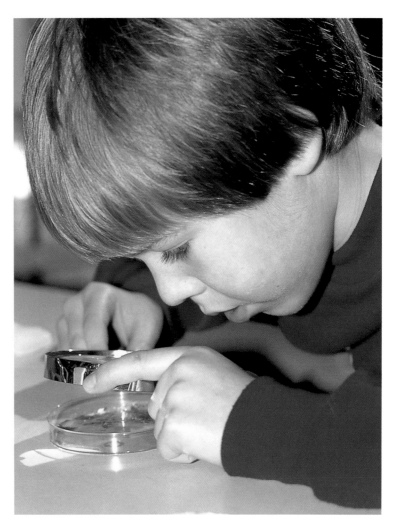

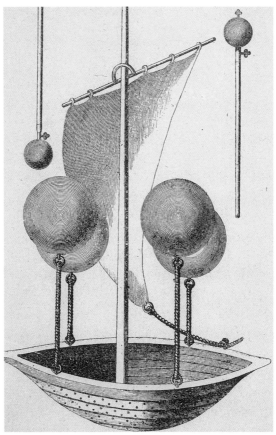

Kuhn illustrates how the dominance of what he calls 'normal science' is established through the uncritical teaching of the reigning scientific outlook. An example of shorter periods of change was Newton's theory of gravity.

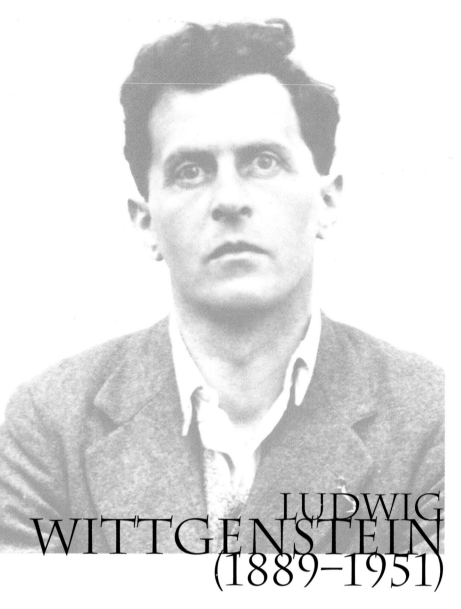

LUDWIG WITTGENSTEIN (1889–1951)

Ludwig Wittgenstein was one of the true geniuses of the 20th century. His genius transcends his status as a philosopher just as Einstein's transcended his status as a scientist. When he published his first book, *Tractatus Logico-philosophicus*, in 1921, few philosophers were willing to conceive of the end of philosophy, but this is what Wittgenstein believed he had achieved. After radically altering his philosophical views in *Philosophical Investigations*, Wittgenstein brought the end of philosophy even closer and transformed Western philosophy irreversibly. Many modern commentators continue to argue that after Wittgenstein all philosophy is futile.

VIENNA – MANCHESTER – CAMBRIDGE

Wittgenstein's life and character bear many of the stereotypical hallmarks of the genius. He was insular, moody, single-minded and prone to erratic behaviour. Wittgenstein was born in Vienna to wealthy parents but always refused the comfort of their financial support. After studying aeronautics at Manchester University, Wittgenstein went to Cambridge to study philosophy. For several years he had been privately writing philosophy and he was encouraged to pursue his interest further by the famous German philosopher, Frege. Soon after arriving he took Cambridge by storm. Bertrand Russell, then a professor at Cambridge, recognised Wittgenstein's talent and took him under his wing only to find very quickly that his protégé threatened to become his philosophical master. Wittgenstein's brilliantly destructive approach to philosophy left Russell uncertain about his own work and their relationship became difficult and intense. Wittgenstein was increasingly uncomfortable at Cambridge and after two years of teaching in Norway he joined the Austrian Army during the First World War. Following this he published his first book called *Tractatus Logico–Philosophicus* (1921) and once again took the philosophical world by storm. However, Wittgenstein's neurotic perfectionism meant that his most important work, *Philosophical Investigations*, wasn't published until two years after his death in 1953.

THE PROBLEM WITH PHILOSOPHY

In *Tractatus Logico–Philosophicus*, Wittgenstein challenges the study of philosophy. He argues that philosophical problems are mostly pseudo-problems. They are problems arrived at in an attempt to push thought beyond the

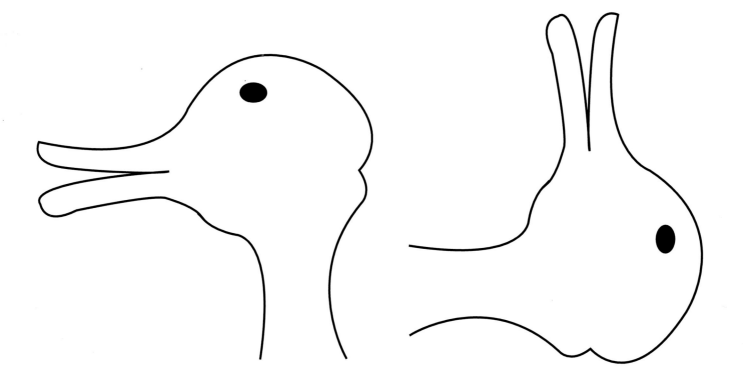

limits imposed upon it by language. For Wittgenstein, the world of facts, which is reality, is contained within, rather than beyond, or below the logical structure of language. There is no world of truth which language represents, because all possibilities for truthful propositions are contained within the logical structure of everyday language. Any attempt to step outside the logical confines of language and establish 'a priori' philosophical certainties is futile because it assumes that language can be pushed beyond its limits.

LANGUAGE GAMES

In *Philosophical Investigations*, Wittgenstein resisted his earlier attempts in *Tractatus Logico–Philosophicus* to push philosophy to the ends of language and understand the limits of factual discourse. He rejected the idea that meaning in language could be accounted for beyond the often multiple nature of its empirical usage. For Wittgenstein, the meaning of words and sentences cannot be understood through a higher logic. Rather words, sentences and their meanings are relational. That is, their meaning is only verified by the nature of their relationship to other words and sentences, which take the shape of familiar language patterns. This

THE ABOVE REPRESENTS A FIGURE THAT ON THE LEFT CAN BE SEEN AS A DUCK AND ON THE RIGHT A RABBIT. WITTGENSTEIN USED THE AMBIGUOUS FIGURE OF THE 'DUCK-RABBIT' TO ILLUSTRATE HOW HUMAN PERCEPTION IS NOT A GIVEN/OBJECTIVE PROCESS. IT SHOWS HOW HUMAN PERCEPTION IS EFFECTED BY THE INTERNAL PICTURE WE CREATE RATHER THAN THOSE CREATED BY THE OBJECT.

means that language can be understood as a complex network of overlapping games played by the interlocutors.

For Wittgenstein, claims to truth can only be assessed by the relative degree of agreement that exists about the rules used to verify them. That is, it is this level of agreement rather than the 'objective' truth itself that counts. 'It is what human beings say that is true and false; and they agree in the language they use. That is not agreement in opinions but in forms of life.' In other words, to say that the propositions or statements made by human beings are initially opinions is to say that they can be verified by their actual meanings. Statements and propositions are, in fact, moves in a game which are verified by the rules of the game. So that the question 'What is a word really?' is analogous to 'What is a piece in Chess?'

Lâcheté des gardes municipaux.   arrêtez.... arrêtez!....   résistance du peuple à l'oppr

Liberté!... Liberté!... chérie combats avec les défenseurs.   mes amis saluons le Christ! C'est notre ma

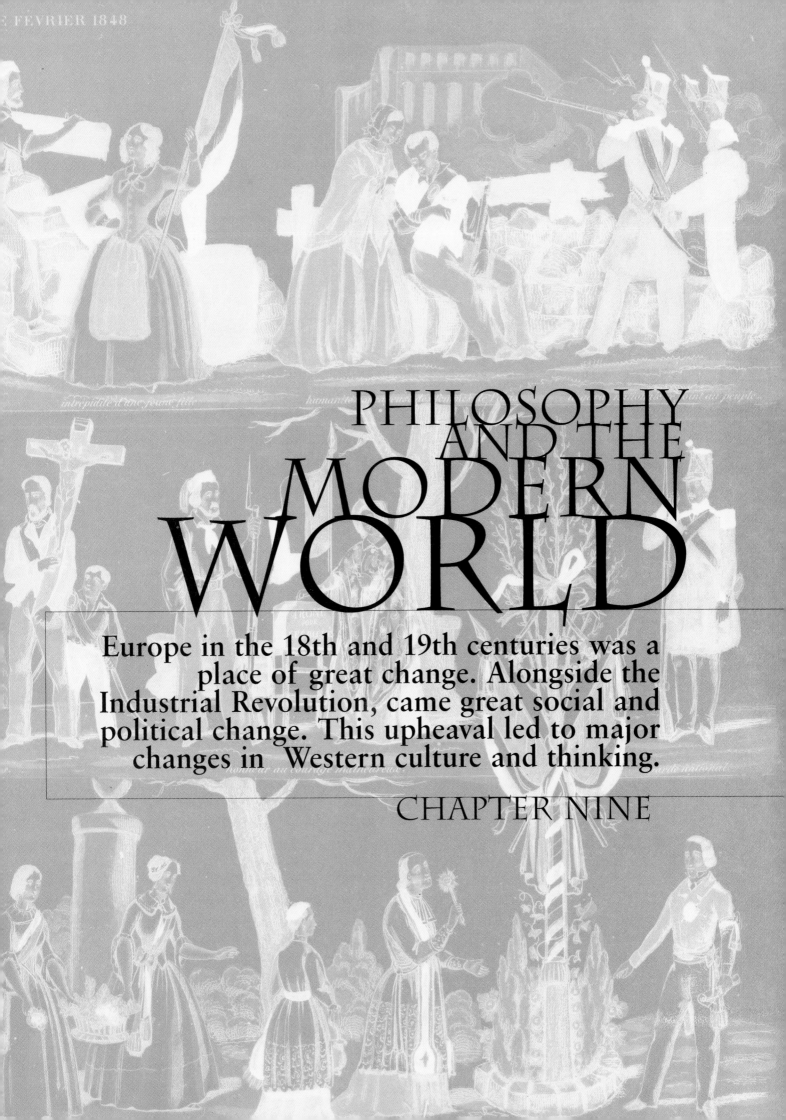

PHILOSOPHY AND THE MODERN WORLD

Europe in the 18th and 19th centuries was a place of great change. Alongside the Industrial Revolution, came great social and political change. This upheaval led to major changes in Western culture and thinking.

CHAPTER NINE

INDUSTRIALISATION AND DEMOCRACY

The Industrial Revolution was responsible for the most dramatic change in the lives of human beings that history has ever seen. The range and possibilities of human experience changed so markedly during this period that a simultaneous change in social and philosophical values was inevitable. In particular, the Industrial Revolution radically changed the organisation of human communities.

MAN AND MACHINE

The Industrial Revolution effected much more than a material change in lifestyle. It has even been argued that the material changes brought about by the Revolution resulted in the internalisation of particular values which prevent contemporaries from fully understanding what went before. According to this view, man internalised means-to-end-values; this is the notion that little of value could exist outside the realm of usefulness. During the Enlightenment, scientific reasoning, which provided the

intellectual foundations of the Industrial Revolution, reached only a small section of society. The Industrial Revolution brought those values to society at large and they became foil for matters of moral and political legitimacy. Moral values, for example, which pre-dated the Revolution, became instruments of necessity for social order and economic progress rather than an end in themselves after the Revolution.

LIBERALISM

The Industrial Revolution also demanded a political system which was able to administer an industrial nation as opposed to a collection of agricultural communities. The political doctrine behind the necessary political reform was Liberalism. The philosophy of Liberalism is not a fixed doctrine, but its exponents do have key beliefs in common. The belief that all political ends must begin with the idea of the natural autonomy of the individual is central to Liberalism. All forms of political organisation must incorporate the right of the individual to pursue his or her own interests. However, the pursuit of those interests cannot be unlimited; rather it should be limited in order to protect the individual. To achieve this, society must be based upon the establishment of 'contracts', for example the contract between the people and the state, i.e. the constitutional state. The type of democracy favoured by liberals is often called 'protective democracy', because its aim is to protect the rights of the individual. The key problem for Liberalism is how to reconcile the need for a state which is powerful enough to protect rights, with the need also to protect people from a powerful state which might abuse those rights. The Industrial Revolution made this problem more pressing, as a more powerful state was needed to cope with greater and more complex responsibilities.

ABOVE RIGHT: THE EARLY DEVELOPMENT OF
A RAIL NETWORK WAS A MAJOR FACTOR IN
EUROPE'S RAPID INDUSTRIAL PROGRESS.
ABOVE: THE EMERGENCE OF FACTORIES AND
NEW HOMES FOR WORKERS CHANGED THE
THE DAY-TO-DAY EXPERIENCES OF THE
MAJORITY OF THE POPULATION. PHILOSOPHY,
TOO, WAS READY FOR CHANGE.

IMPERIALISM

The emergence of the liberal democratic state carried with it many contradictions. Chief among them was imperialism. The liberal democratic state depended upon the myths of nationhood for its legitimacy. The duty of the citizens to donate a larger share of wealth to the state needed to be upheld by more than just the coercive powers of the state. Nationalism performed that function by generating the sense that citizens had a duty to serve their nation. An essential aspect of nationalism was also its depiction of other nations as either inferior or enemies. This process helped nations maintain a strong sense of identity; the citizen's responsibilities to his or her nation were made stronger by the continual threat of other nations. Nationalism, upon which the liberal democratic state was dependent, therefore, was one of the forces behind the obsessive imperialism of the dominant European powers in the 19th century. The other motivating factor was, of course, economic. Without its enormous empire, Britain would not have been the spearhead of the Industrial Revolution.

Why, in the past 200 years, has the human race been more intent on its own self-destruction than at any other comparable period of human history? How is it that this period of self-destruction has also given us democracy and human rights? Can we be certain that this period of self-destruction is coming to an end? These and other such pressing questions have been of central concern to philosophers who have sought to look deeper into the human condition of the modern world.

TOTAL WAR

War has always been a fundamental aspect of the human condition. In 1832 its most famous philosophical investigator, Karl Von Clausewitz, wrote his treatise *On War*. He spoke of a new type of war called *total war*. This term referred, in the main, to Napoleon. He argued that logically war would reach its conclusion in the total war of nation versus nation, whereby the only end can be the total defeat of the peoples and armies of a whole nation. Clausewitz believed that the destructiveness of this perennial aspect of the human condition was thereby reaching its limits. However, after the period 1914–1945 the brutal limits of the human capacity for self-destruction were in need of re-evaluation. After the unprecedented destruction of the First World War through to the devastation of Hiroshima in 1945, humankind was forced to recognise the possibility of its total annihilation.

NATIONALISM

From its birth in the French Revolution of 1789, nationalism has taken on both negative

WAR AND DICTATORSHIP

'Let us not hear of Generals who conquer without bloodshed. If a bloody slaughter is a horrible sight, then that is a ground for paying more respect to War, but not for making the sword we wear blunter and blunter by degrees from feelings of humanity, until some one steps in with one that is sharp and lops off the arm from our body.'
Karl Von Clausewitz, 1832.

THE SPANISH CIVIL WAR WAS MORE THAN A CONFLICT BETWEEN FASCISM AND ITS ENEMIES. IT WAS A CONFLICT OF ALL THE DIFFERENT IDEOLOGIES OF AN UNCERTAIN EUROPE.

ABOVE: MUSSOLINI VISITS ADOLF HITLER IN 1937. THE ITALIAN TOOK ADVANTAGE OF DEEP-ROOTED ECONOMIC PROBLEMS AS HE ROSE TO POWER.
LEFT: STALIN'S BRUTAL REGIME GREATLY AFFECTED THE CULTURE AND CRITICAL DISPOSITION OF 20TH CENTURY EUROPE.

and positive forms. One of the earliest and most famous accounts of nationalism came from Italian philosopher Giuseppe Mazzini, who attempted to give it a positive gloss. He believed that all nations whose peoples had a common language and culture had a certain spirit and a mission to contribute, in particular ways, to human progress. Mazzini viewed nationalism as a progressive force but its regressive character has also been much evident. Nietzsche, Schopenhauer, Heidegger and other 19th and early 20th century philosophers were greatly affected by the idea of the nation. The nation for them was much more than just an empirical fact, it was an essential medium of human experience and progress. Nowadays the idea of the nation is so in-grained in our everyday beliefs about human identity that it is almost considered a natural phenomenon. This is unsurprising considering the degree to which the idea of nationhood has dominated the 20th century experience. But, as the contemporary philosopher Beni-dict Anderson argues, 'its recency as an idea belies its status as a natural condition'.

For Anderson, the nation is a community that exists solely in our imagination.

THE TERROR OF THE TOTAL STATE

For many contemporary philosophers, the modern world reached its final, logical destination in the horrific rationality of the concentration camps of Hitler's Germany and Stalin's Russia. Concentration camps represented the modern idea of the 'purification' of society according to a particular ideal. They employed increasingly powerful instruments of state machinery. The most significant investigations of the total state are in the main literary rather than philosophical. George Orwell's *1984*, Solzhenitsyn's *Gulag Archipelago*, Primo Levi's *The Drowned and the Saved* and Milan Kundera's *The Joke* show the wealth of literature on this subject. These and other accounts of the horrors of the total state had an enormous impact upon scholarship in general. The work of some of the most important philosophers since the Second World War was written under the shadow of the terrible atrocities carried out in the name of ideology.

ADAM SMITH
(1723–90)

It is widely assumed that Adam Smith's most famous work, *The Wealth of Nations*, contains the philosophy which underpins the economic values of liberal capitalism. However, like many of the great dead philosophers, Smith is more often cited than read and debate about the nature and consequences of his writing has obscured his ideas. Whether one is inclined to favour his views or not, Smith's writing is much more than economic theory. It encompasses ethics, political theory and history.

MORALITY

The book which initially made Smith famous, *The Theory of Moral Sentiments*, was published in 1759 but is rarely read today. Its philosophical basis was indebted to the age of scientific reason and its method was thoroughly empirical. Smith argued that experience alone teaches us that people are naturally inclined to selfishness. He went on to state that those aspects of human nature which incline people towards social co-operation offer an insufficient guarantee for social harmony. Therefore a state authority is vitally necessary. However, social harmony can be achieved by ensuring that the interests to which men dedicate themselves, often self-ishly, coincide with those that promote social harmony. The activities that Smith had in mind were work and the protection of private property.

ABOVE: THE PHILOSOPHY OF ADAM SMITH IS OFTEN READ AS A BLUEPRINT FOR LIBERAL CAPITALISM. HOWEVER, HIS WORK CONTAINS MUCH MORE SUBTLE REFLECTION ON MORALITY AND ETHICS.

THE INVISIBLE HAND

At the time it was written, Adam Smith's economic theory was extremely radical. In mid-18th century Britain the spirit of capitalism was firmly established but economic practice had its roots buried within aristocratic privilege. Smith was highly critical of privilege and monopolistic practices because he firmly believed that they restricted the natural spirit of enterprise which can only be achieved through free competition. For Smith, free competition encourages both enterprise and economic progress and produces the best possible distribution of value upon goods and labour. He likened the consequences of a free market to an invisible hand which places the equilibrium value upon goods and labour. Smith's ideal of the free market led him to a minimalist view of the role of the state. He saw the state as merely necessary to preserve the free market by protecting it from privilege and monopoly. He was sceptical about the ability of governments to produce greater economic progress by regulating the economy: 'No regulation of commerce can increase the quantity of industry in any society beyond what its capital can maintain. It can only divert a part of it into a direction into which it might not otherwise have gone...' For Smith, there is no reason to expect that direction to be an advantageous one.

THE WEALTH OF SMITH'S PHILOSOPHY

Adam Smith's legacy has been enormous. His ideas are now so well known and practised that they are regarded as the basis of the economic thinking which has dominated Western beliefs concerning social and economic progress. His view of competitive rationality has also found its way into a great deal of philosophical discourse. However, one must be extremely careful when reading Adam Smith's work when looking for the principles which have shaped the political and social progress of the West. This is due to the fact that his notion of the ideal relationship between state and society was ignored by the Western world in favour of a state that became ever more powerful and regulative.

JOHN STUART MILL (1806–73)

The problem of how to reconcile individual freedom with the freedom of others and the well-being of society has never been far from political debate. J. S. Mill focused on this problem more than any of his predecessors. The philosophy he built provided the foundation for an approach to social and political matters which has become mainstream in the 20th century. This approach regards individual interest and happiness as the starting point for all considerations of the institutions of government and society.

A PHILOSOPHICAL FAMILY

J. S. Mill's father, James Mill, was a founder of Utilitarianism. John was educated by his father and, although he tried to move away from the Utilitarian creed, his father's work is evident in his J. S. Mill's writings. While employed for the East India Company in London J. S. Mill wrote his most important work *On Liberty, Representative Government and Utilitarianism*. From 1865 to 1868 J. S . Mill was a Member of Parliament with the Radical party, with whom he campaigned for women's suffrage and radical economic reform.

ON LIBERTY

For J. S. Mill the principle of liberty is sacrosanct. The right of every individual to choose his or her own fate is absolute and is only forgone when the actions of that individual cause harm to another individual. 'That the only purpose for which power can be rightfully exercised over that member of a civilised community, against his will, is to prevent harm to others. His own good, either physical or moral, is not a sufficient warrant.' However, the idea that societies and governments simply tolerate individuality was not enough for J. S. Mill. According to J. S. Mill, a good and progressive society not only tolerates individu-

ality it harnesses the freedom of the individual as a right and an instrument for advancing civilisation. The political freedom that comes with freedom of expression and suffrage is conducive to developing the moral character of individuals and thus of society: 'In proportion to the development of his individuality, each person becomes more valuable to himself, and is, therefore, capable of being more valuable to others.' Additionally, by increasing the scope of independent thought, reason and rationality are advanced.

J. S. Mill was a fervent defender of women's rights and he was keen to see both sexes involved in the political process. He argued that women's participation was vital to curb male self-interest which he thought would overwhelm the interests of the family and therefore society and every individual.

GOOD GOVERNMENT

For J. S. Mill, government and the rule of law are essential to protect liberty, but government is also the chief threat to liberty. This threat to liberty comes from government's tendency to over-extend its powers for its own preservtion. Liberty can also be threatened by a concern to

satisfy the wishes of the public. For J. S. Mill, the rise of public opinion is the source of this threat, which at its most persuasive can restrict individuality. The ideal form of government, according to J. S. Mill, was representative democracy. In a modern, complex and crowded society, representative, rather than direct, democracy is ideal because it protects governments from being influenced by a largely ignorant mass, whilst retaining sufficient mechanisms to check government power. Many of J. S. Mill's predecessors had tried to protect tradition from democracy or protect democracy from tradition, but J. S. Mill wanted to protect democracy from democracy. The sum of this equation is liberal democracy; the form of government assumed by J .S. Mill's native Britain and, at one time or another, by most of the Western world.

MAX WEBER (1864–1920)

Max Weber was responsible for the most comprehensive theory of the origins and nature of modernity. His insights even exceed those of Marx. Max Weber was a social scientist but his intellectual contribution spills over into many areas, including philosophy.

A POLITICIAN'S SON

Weber was born in Erfurt, Germany, in 1864. His father was a politician, and as a result Weber came to understand this vocation more perceptively than any other 20th century thinker. After completing his military service in the army (where his taste for duelling and drinking was a huge benefit) Weber finished his university exams in law. In 1894 he became Professor of Economics at Freibur University. At this time Weber's life was characterised by either intense intellectual activity or manic depression. After a long period of travelling in the late 1890s, Weber recovered from his poor mental health and in 1904 published the first part of *The Protestant Ethic and the Spirit of Capitalism*. The second part was largely inspired by a visit to America where he saw the

growth of modern bureaucracy, a constant theme in his work, in its most progressive state. After the First World War he helped draft Germany's Weimar constitution.

CAPITALISM AND THE WEST

In *The Protestant Ethic and the Spirit of Capitalism* Weber explains why capitalism developed in the West. Weber, unlike Marx, did not see human history as a consequence of class conflict and its material conditions. Instead, Weber emphasised the social culture and values which lead to particular economic and political practices. For Weber, if we want to understand the growth of capitalism in the West we must consider the uniqueness of Western culture. The factor most unique to the West was its social values which emerged

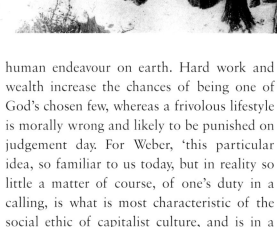

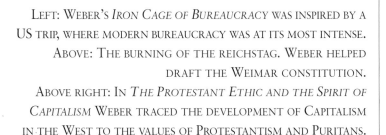

from the dominant religions of the 16th and 17th centuries, when capitalism developed. These values were characteristic of Protestantism, in particular its more extreme form, Puritanism. Merchants and traders in the 16th and 17th centuries, many of whom were Protestant or Puritan, had a particular attitude towards the accumulation of wealth. Instead of acquiring wealth in order to live a luxurious lifestyles, Protestant traders reinvested their wealth, worked hard and were frugal. A key feature of Protestantism was the belief that God is best served, not only by worship, but also by one's contribution to

human endeavour on earth. Hard work and wealth increase the chances of being one of God's chosen few, whereas a frivolous lifestyle is morally wrong and likely to be punished on judgement day. For Weber, 'this particular idea, so familiar to us today, but in reality so little a matter of course, of one's duty in a calling, is what is most characteristic of the social ethic of capitalist culture, and is in a sense the fundamental basis of it'. Nowhere was this spirit more prevalent than America.

BUREAUCRACY AND DEMOCRACY

Weber saw bureaucracy as the most significant feature of the organisation of human communities to emerge from the capitalist spirit. All successful civilisations, from the Ancient Greeks to the modern Japanese, have had bureaucratic systems of control. Recent Western civilisation has even enhanced the rationalising potential of bureaucracy through technological achievements. The unrelenting demand for efficiency, characteristic of the capitalist spirit and underpinned by technical expertise, has fuelled the growth of large-scale organisations which dominate modern life. Weber regarded the state as a unique feature of the development of the modern West. The total domination of the means of violence, which is necessary for the existence of the modern state, is unparalleled in history. Based on this foundation, the state has taken on forms of bureaucratic organisation. In the bureaucratic state politics becomes a vocation, a job for the professional rather than the idealist. Like other professionals, politicians are affected by their responsibilities as part of a social organisation. Weber knew the potential undesirable features of the bureaucratic state; i.e. the centralisation of power and the denial of individuality, but he saw trends towards the further rationalization of society as inevitable.

Karl Schmitt was one of the most brilliant and compelling of 20th century thinkers. Writing in a century which has seen human conflict pushed to its limits, Schmitt's philosophy contains few illusions about the political limits of human co-operation. Born in 1888, a year later than Hitler, Schmitt's notoriety as a philosopher is compounded by his active support for Nazism during Hitler's reign in Germany. His allegiance to National Socialism did not represent a departure from his philosophy, but even the most liberal of democratic philosophers have been forced to confront Schmitt's arguments.

KARL SCHMITT (1888-1985)

CATHOLIC BEGINNINGS

Karl Schmitt was born in Westphalia, Germany, in 1888, to strongly Catholic parents who hoped their son would join the priesthood. Without rejecting his family's Catholicism, Schmitt decided instead of going to university to study law after the First World war forced him to ask uncomfortable questions about the highly moral ideals he had inherited from Catholicism. After the War and during the reign of the Weimar republic, Schmitt established his reputation as a scholar with his three most important works – *Political Theology* (1922), *The Crisis of Parliamentary Democracy* (1923) and *The Concept of the Political* (1932). The acute political realism, which he displayed in his writing, led him to make a choice between support for Hitler or chaos. He chose Hitler and his reputation as a scholar has never completely recovered, even though in recent years Schmitt's work has become fashionable.

FRIENDS AND ENEMIES

The main target of Schmitt's realism is the liberal-constitutional understanding of the state and the parliamentary conception of politics that underpins it. For Schmitt, politics is not the activity and deliberation by representatives who construct laws to which the state and its citizens are bound. Such an understanding of politics suffers from the illusion that the object of political struggle is truth. For Schmitt, authority, order and the definition of who one's enemies and friends are in the struggle to control scarce resources is the aim of political life. Consequently, every 'religious, moral economic, ethical or other antithesis transforms itself into a political one if it is sufficiently strong to group human beings effectively according to friend and enemy'. According to Schmitt there is simply no exception to the rule that what matters in politics is the definition of who one's friends and enemies are. When political struggle is intense, when it results in violent conflict one's enemies are stripped of their humanity in order that they can be destroyed. To ignore this essential condition of political life by believing that truth and justice come before authority is to court with the possibility that the perennial struggle between friends and enemies will lead to violent conflict.

Therefore, total political authority is indispensable to any society that seeks responsible harmony. The state must be able to deal with exceptional circumstances, i.e. crises in the political struggles of friends and enemies either internally or externally. For Schmitt, 'the sovereign is he who decides on the exception.' – i.e. the point at which the state overrides the constraints of the law by which it is normally bound.

ABOVE: THE BRUTAL TRENCH CONFLICTS OF THE FIRST WORLD WAR MADE SCHMITT QUESTION HIS CATHOLICISM.
ABOVE RIGHT: SCHMITT'S ASSOCIATION WITH HITLER HAS MADE HIM A CONTROVERSIAL FIGURE IN MODERN PHILOSOPHY.

ORDER OR JUSTICE?

Those who hold strong belief in the ideals of democracy would do well to consider Schmitt's analysis because if you take it to its logical conclusions democracy can never be anything more than a practice which secures legitimacy for the state to maintain order. Ideals of equality and justice will always be subservient to this fact and will therefore never be fully realised.

Simone de Beauvoir was the first systematic feminist philosopher. Her famous book, The Second Sex, published in 1949, gave a philosophical account of the development of patriarchal society and the condition of women within it. The impact of The Second Sex was immense; it considerably altered the whole approach to philosophical and political issues about women. Much of the supposedly pro-woman literature that preceded de Beauvoir concentrated on the interests of women as a part of a family, rather than as an individual. De Beauvoir used the philosophy of Existentialism, which she had developed alongside her partner Jean-Paul Sartre, to reveal the unacceptable weight of women's subordination throughout history.

SIMONE DE BEAUVOIR (1908–86)

A LIFE OF PHILOSOPHY

Born in Paris in 1908, de Beauvoir graduated, along with Jean-Paul Sartre, at the Sorbonne University in Paris. After leaving university she taught in Marseilles and Paris. Her literary and philosophical output was extensive; she was also a novelist. Throughout her life and career as a philosopher her relationship with Sartre was characterised by the burdens of womanhood which provided the focus for her work. As a result, there has been extensive consideration of the relationship between her life and work, to which de Beauvoir contributed with her four-volume autobiography.

A WOMAN'S EXISTENCE

As an existentialist de Beauvoir believed that human beings are responsible for the meanings which they and others attach to their lives. Though we are all thrown into a world that has established norms and values we inform our own choices – each individual is

> IN *THE SECOND SEX* DE BEAUVOIR REVEALED 'THE UNACCEPTABLE WEIGHT OF WOMEN'S SUBORDINATION THROUGHOUT HISTORY'.

essentially his or her own world. 'A living being is nothing else but what it does…essence does not precede existence: in its pure subjectivity, the human being is nothing.' De Beauvoir continued '…what defines the situation of women in a remarkable way is that while being an autonomous freedom, along with every human creature, she discovers herself and chooses herself in a world where men oblige her to accept herself as the Other'. What de Beauvoir means by 'the Other' is critical to her whole philosophy. For de Beauvoir men have historically defined themselves as the essential being – the being who most completely embodies the faculties which make human beings distinct from animals, i.e. rationality. Therefore, women have been conceived as the Other of man, who is the central medium of humanity.

Throughout human history, women's status as the Other has been cemented in the cultural institutions of patriarchal domination, i.e. marriage and the family. For de Beauvoir: 'You are not born a woman: you become one.' She describes how the institution of marriage is 'obscene' because it denies women's individuality, which is the essential basis of human freedom. What should be a spontaneous and equal partnership of love becomes in marriage a contract of subjugation where the woman is bound by her unavoidable duties as a wife. In any case, the very notion of male fidelity in marriage is inconceivable. An authentic exitence, one which necessarily encounters risk and adventure, would be incompatible with perfect fidelity.

EMANCIPATION OF THE INDIVIDUAL

De Beauvoir's existentialism, i.e. her belief in every human being's unshakeable freedom to impose their authentic meaning upon their own life, leads her to a problematic position on feminist strategy. Essentially, she must argue that women consent to the tyranny that men have imposed on their individuality. De Beauvoir did not think that women's freedom lay in simply attacking men and she distanced herself from the American feminists of the 1960s. For de Beauvoir, women's freedom can ultimately only be found through their capacity for individuality. To rely simply upon attacking men would not relieve them of this. Groups dedicated to the emancipation of women should concentrate on removing those institutions which restrict women's freedom.

THE FRANKFURT SCHOOL

The group of philosophers which became known as the Frankfurt School was brought together by the formation of the Institute of Social Research in 1929. The Frankfurt school does not provide a single philosophical outlook and this is in part because it is influenced by so many diverse thinkers – Marx, Freud, Nietzsche, Max Weber. The declared aim of the school gives a clue as to why such diverse influences were necessary. In 1931 the director of the school, Max Horkheimer, set out this aim in his inaugural address. He stated that he wanted to develop a new approach to the study of human experience, one which synthesised the concrete concerns of the social sciences with the more abstract and universal pursuits of philosophy. The idea instigated by the school was not so much a particular philosophy as a programme.

JEWISH MIGRANTS ARRIVE IN AMERICA IN THE 1930S. THE FRANKFURT SCHOOL WERE ALSO FORCED TO FLEE THEIR EUROPEAN BASE UNDER THREAT FROM THE NAZIS. IN THE US THEY FORMED A LONG-RUNNING ASSOCIATION WITH UCLA.

CRITICAL THEORY

One of the main motivating factors behind the programme was the antipathy which members of the Frankfurt school felt towards the work of the Vienna school. The philosophy of the Vienna school, i.e. positivism, held human beings to be mere facts or objects, whose actions and behaviour could be calculated scientifically. According to this view, the facts of human existence could be separated from the values attributed to it. For the Vienna school, philosophical speculation about the political significance of received views of human nature was meaningless. However, the Frankfurt school disagreed and argued that this view is an ideological one because the views about human existence which it deems scientific are merely those which constitute the facts which are essential for capitalism. The Frankfurt School sought to develop a new way of studying society, called critical theory, which was wary of not seeking normative and practical explanation at the expense of philosophical reflection.

THE NEW LEFT

In 1933, after the election of Hitler in Germany, the Frankfurt School went into exile in America. Events in Germany instigated the first significant product of the School, *The Dialectic of Enlightenment*, written by Theodore Adorno and Max Horkheimer.

Adorno and Horkheimer argued that science and technology were, apart from being bearers of human progress, sinking humanity into a 'new kind of barbarism'. The barbarism to which Adorno and Horkheimer refer is not inflicted by the ruling class elites, but by a new technological consciousness which has gripped mass society.

The striking feature of this technological consciousness is the constant attempt to totally dominate human beings. In other words, a 'totally administered society' in which human beings are increasingly dehumanised. Even though one of the Frankfurt School's strongest influences was Marxism its members believed that the political systems created in the name of Marxism were just as responsible for dehumanising our existence as those created in the name of capitalism. It is this political position which came to constitute the so-called New Left which was dominant in the 1960s and 70s.

ABOVE: THEODORE ADORNO SPOKE OF 'A NEW KIND OF BARBARISM' INFECTING HUMANITY. RIGHT: MAX HORKHEIMER TRIED TO COMBINE THE CONCRETE CONCERNS OF THE SOCIAL SCIENCES WITH THE ABSTRACT CONCERNS OF PHILOSOPHY.

The ideological conflicts which engulfed the West between the two World Wars were transformed into an acute opposition between capitalism and Communism after the Second World War. Social and political tensions prevalent before the Second World War were repressed by an age of consumerism and welfare which absorbed potential discontent. For many social and political philosophers, the consumer society signalled a new phase in the development of the west and in particular capitalism and liberal democracy. Herbert Marcuse was one of the first social philosophers to recognise the potential significance of a changing West. In his most famous book, *One-Dimensional Man*, Marcuse produced a comprehensive indictment of what he described as the 'comfortable, smooth, reasonable, democratic unfreedom' of industrial civilisation.

HERBERT MARCUSE (1898–1979)

FROM FREIBURG TO FRANKFURT SCHOOL

Marcuse's philosophical education began at the University of Freiburg alongside Heidegger and Husserl. However, unlike Heidegger, Marcuse, who was born to a Jewish family, fled Germany for Geneva and later New York. His exile was comforted by his membership of the famous Frankfurt Institute for Social Research which he worked with in America until 1940. In the 1940s Marcuse worked for the US government, employing his knowledge of European Fascism and central European politics in the fight against Nazism. After this, Marcuse stayed in the US, teaching at Columbia and Harvard Universities.

AS A MEMBER OF THE FAMOUS FRANKFURT INSTITUTE FOR SOCIAL RESEARCH, HERBERT MARCUSE WROTE AGAINST WHAT HE SAW AS AN OPPRESSIVE TECHNOLOGICAL SOCIETY.

ONE-DIMENSIONAL MAN

Marcuse's approach to social philosophy is a synthesis of Marx, Freud and Hegel. Marx's emphasis on man's relationship to production as the basis of human history is retained and explored in the light of more advanced capitalism. Marcuse also employs Hegel's dialectic. He says: 'It is the rationality of contradiction, of the opposition of forces, tendencies, elements, which constitutes the movement of the real and, if comprehended, the concept of the real.' Organisational progress in human societies is driven by an opposition of forces, i.e. between classes and competing descriptions of the ideal society. However, in Western societies, that opposition of forces is suppressed to the detriment of advancing the most rational way of organising communities.

In *One-Dimensional Man*, Marcuse argues that the aspects of Western society which are most valued are the instruments of oppression rather than progress. Western society also places a high value upon economic freedom, which produced consumerism, and political freedom in the form of liberal democracy. He says that the economic rationality of advanced capitalism is based on falsifying people's real needs in order to maintain a market system of production and consumption. This system is now so advanced that intellectual and economic creativity and productivity are channelled through the consumption of largely irrational and wasteful leisure pursuits, such as sport. For Marcuse, the entertainment of the masses helps to suppress more rational ways of organising societies. Social discontent, which ought to be prevalent considering the slavery of labour, is quelled through ever-increasing expansion of consumption. This repression of any potential for opposing the prevailing system is also upheld in the illusory practice of political freedom. Political freedom is reduced to a choice, at elections, of indistinguishable political representatives, who engage in inconsequential, technical debates which are exaggerated to effect the illusion of a working democracy. Modern society is therefore one-dimensional. For Marcuse 'this society is irrational as a whole. Its productivity is destructive of the free development of human needs and faculties, its peace maintained by the constant threat of war, its growth dependent on the repression of the real possibilities for pacifying the struggle for existence – individual, national, and international'.

ABOVE: FOR MARCUSE, BY CONSUMING ACTIVITIES LIKE BASEBALL THE MASSES ARE LESS INCLINED TO REFLECT UPON THE SOCIAL AND POLITICAL CONDITIONS OF THE WORLD THEY LIVE IN.
BELOW: MARCUSE USES FREUD'S ARGUMENT THAT CIVILISATION IS BASED ON A CONSTANT REPRESSION OF HUMAN INSTINCT, OR EROS (LIFE INSTINCT).

HANNAH ARENDT (1906–75)

Between 1914 and 1945 Europe endured a period of unprecedented turmoil. The social and political conditions which gave Hitler and Stalin the platform for their tyranny reveal much about the human condition. Hannah Arendt was the first philosopher to recognise the extent to which the events of the early 20th century transcend their gruesome history and stand as a frightening, albeit extreme, reflection on the state of humanity. But Arendt's work has a wider significance and she is one of the most original thinkers of the 20th century. Even though she is principally a political philosopher, the scope of her thinking is not encumbered by the limits political philosophy had placed upon itself at the time she was writing. Arendt's chief concern is with the nature of the political community and its moral values, within which citizens think and act. In this way she is a political philosopher, but in her analysis she also brings to bear classical philosophy, social theory and history.

Born to Jewish parents in Hanover, Germany, in 1906, Arendt's life was directly affected by the condition she studied. In 1933, soon after receiving her doctorate in philosophy from the University of Heidelberg, Arendt was forced into exile after the rise to power of Hitler. After a brief period in Paris, Arendt fled to New York, where she stayed as a professor at the New School for Social Research until her death in 1975.

ARENDT'S LIFE MIRRORED THE CONDITIONS SHE THOUGHT TYPICAL OF LIFE IN THE 20TH CENTURY. IN 1933, BECAUSE OF HER JEWISH BACKGROUND, SHE WAS FORCED INTO EXILE.

THE ORIGINS OF TOTALITARIANISM

In Arendt's study of the conditions which gave rise to the regimes of Hitler and Stalin, entitled *The Origins of Totalitarianism*, she argued that these origins lie in the development of mass society. Industrialisation and imperialist economic expansion created a mass society with a politically inactive majority, whose everyday concerns could be satisfied by immediate material needs. Inexperience of political action and a lack of exposure to different cultures and politics meant that the masses were more receptive to irrational political doctrines such as Nationalism. This condition, together with an increasing detachment from meaningful community life, made Germany and Russia particularly susceptible to totalitarianism.

THE BANALITY OF EVIL

In Arendt's controversial sequel to *The Origins of Totalitarianism*, called *Eichmann in Jerusalem*, she investigated the brutality of the Nazi regime. Arendt was concerned to discover why so many apparently ordinary citizens actively participated in Nazi Germany's mass killings. At his trial Eichmann claimed he was merely following orders while manning the concentration camps and therefore obeying the law as a dutiful citizen. Though Arendt did not excuse Eichmann's actions, she did regard them as a product of the menacing bureaucracy of Hitler's regime. Despite his crimes, Eichmann was frighteningly normal.

THOUGHT AND ACTION

Arendt believed that behaviour like that of Eichmann could be avoided if political structures enabled citizens to participate actively in public power. Exposure to cultural and political plurality and active political interaction can reduce susceptibility to the type of crude certainties of the Nazis.

Arendt maintained a nostalgia for the Ancient Greek Polis. She believed that the ideal of the politically active citizen as an end in itself was lost with Plato's alternative understanding of freedom. Arendt argued that from Plato onwards Western thought regarded freedom as existing outside politics. However,

A KEY ASPECT OF ARENDT'S WORK WAS HER ACCOUNT OF NAZI GENOCIDE. IN *EICHMAN IN JERUSALEM* SHE DESCRIBED HOW WORRYINGLY NORMAL NAZIS LIKE EICHMAN (ABOVE) WERE.

for Arendt the 'raison d'être of politics is freedom and its field of experience is action... Men are free – as distinguished from their possessing the gift of freedom – as long as they act, neither before nor after; for to be free and to act are the same.'

JÜRGEN HABERMAS (1929–)

A LIVING LEGEND

Jürgen Habermas is one of the greatest living philosophers. His work, in terms of its scope, depth and influence, is comparable to the other great philosophers of the modern age, Karl Marx and Max Weber. In the past 20 years, his writing has been so influential that there is an entire industry of Habermas scholars working at universities throughout Europe, North America and beyond. The main reason for Habermas's guru status is that he provides a universal framework for research and discussion which is almost akin to a science. His work has a relevance which extends to the study of linguistics, psychology, media, international relations, political science and of course philosophy. Habermas has been described as 'the last great rationalist' and this is one source of his appeal. In a world which seems increasingly resistant to universal remedies, hopes and certainties of any type, Habermas offers us the chance of a dream invented during the Enlightenment. That dream is the establishment of a science of human relationships which will provide a foundation for the creation of an ideal community.

THE PROJECT OF MODERNITY

In 1981 Habermas wrote an article entitled *Modernity versus Postmodernity*. He declared, against the grain of the most fashionable doctrines, that 'the project of modernity has

ABOVE, LEFT: JÜRGEN HABERMAS HAS BEEN DESCRIBED AS THE 'LAST GREAT RATIONALIST' BECAUSE HE BELIEVES THAT THE POTENTIAL OF THE ENLIGHTENMENT IS YET TO BE REALISED. ABOVE: 18TH-CENTURY COFFEE HOUSE SOCIETY. THE ENLIGHTENMENT INSPIRED HABERMAS'S THINKING.

MUCH OF HABERMAS'S RECENT WORK HAS
CONCERNED ISSUES FACING THE NEW GERMAN
STATE FOLLOWING THE UNIFICATION OF EAST
AND WEST GERMANY IN 1991.

not yet been fulfilled'. By this he meant that the potential for the rationalisation of the world, characteristic of the modern age, had not been fulfilled.

If we take the most universally understood characteristic of the modern world, i.e. means/end rationality, then we are bound to be pessimistic about the potential of producing a more successful way of organising human communities. Under the narrow perspective of means/end rationality human communities are structured around the need to master the world in the name of self-interest. The ideal of gradually expanding the scope for enhancing our capacity to pursue an ever enlarging self-interest comes at a price. The cost is the deterioration of the values which once persuaded us of the need to conform to values and interests outside of ourselves. Religious values, for example, which once helped unify our lives, must be loosened in the pursuit of greater self-interest. During the Enlightenment this price was worth paying because it led to the abandonment of superstition and religious belief to make room for political institutions which catered for a greater diversity of opinions. However, there is soon little of universal value which can provide a basis for action and improve welfare and social understanding.

COMMUNICATIVE ACTION

Habermas does not advocate a return to the dominance of religion, because he wants to preserve much of the social and political progress achieved by the Enlightenment at the expense of religion. Rather, he suggests that we rejuvenate an essential component of the modern world which has been undervalued due to the dominance of means/end rationality. He argues that society should encourage social action which develops and enhances structures which foster greater understanding and communication. This will enhance the possibility of wider agreement about the needs of human communities beyond self-interest. The theory invented by Habermas to justify and realise this aim is called the 'theory of communicative action'. An essential ingredient of this theory is the attempt to explain that our most universal attribute, language, contains within it permanent and universal features which enable wide agreement.

CHALLENGING AN ORDERED WORLD

Postmodernism is a state of mind, it is an attitude. The term was first used in the 1960s to describe the dawning of a new era which Jean François Lyotard described as characterised by the 'gradual decline of the old ideologies and belief systems of the modern world'.

CHAPTER TEN

Bob Dylan made a significant contribution to the blurring of the boundaries between high and low culture. Dylan's poetic lyrics led some to suggest that he should be given comparable status to the great poets.

When philosophy broke its ties with science and theology in the 18th century, it considered itself an arbiter of culture. Disputes about aesthetics, historical accuracy, grammatical correctness, medical ethics and methods of social research were all settled by philosophy. This was because philosophy, apparently, had privileged access to the foundations of human knowledge. In recent years the idea that there is a permanent foundation of human knowledge has been challenged. Similarly, distinctions between the superficial and the meaningful were radically questioned. This resulted in a widespread examination of all cultural hierarchies and led philosophers to move beyond their traditional areas, of logic, metaphysics,

POPULAR CULTURE AND PHILOSOPHY

science and classical literature. The new areas of study include mass and popular culture, i.e. film, popular literature, commercial advertisements and popular music. And from the philosophical study of popular culture a new set of philosophical concepts and ideas emerged.

CULTURAL STUDIES

During the 1980s a new subject area took hold of humanities departments in Europe and America. Commonly called 'Cultural Studies', it concerned itself with the study of identity. For the postmodern philosopher Jacques Derrida, the question of identity pervades humanity. He argued that the ways we define and identify ourselves within communities provide the context for our understanding of

Mass and popular culture is an important area of study for the modern philosopher. Nowhere is modern culture more clearly represented than The Mall.

morality and truth. Moral, rational and scientific progress are not separate from the cultural identities from which they were created. Popular culture is nothing if it is not the expression of certain identities in various forms, which, no matter how banal, express moral, political and philosophical views. From Madonna to Oprah Winfrey, popular culture is filled with images and ideas that contain a philosophical resonance.

ATTITUDE AND IRONY

Postmodern philosophy is the source of much of the new concern with popular culture. The postmodern attitude embraces diversity and rejects the idea that a rational belief system can claim authority over all others. But this attitude also has a negative side. Postmodernism can reflect cynicism in a world regarded as increasingly chaotic and out of control. This cynicism is often expressed in fatalistic irony or ironic parody.

MEDIA ICONS ARE A KEY PART OF MODERN CULTURE. MANY CONTEMPORARY PHILOSOPHERS ARE JUST AS COMFORTABLE WRITING ABOUT MADONNA AS THEY ARE ABOUT POLITICS OR THE CLASSICS.

ART AND CULTURE

Although postmodern art and culture predates the postmodern philosophy it is part of the same movement. For example, postmodern architecture reflects a rejection of the ordered and symmetrical architecture of the 19th and much of the 20th century. In fine art, pop art represented an ironic parody of popular culture and a rejection of purist conceptions of art. Films such as *Eraserhead* and *Dune* have depicted cynicism and ironic indifference. And the introduction of non-white and non-Western authors into school and university curricula shows the increased influence of Postmodern thinking.

TECHNOLOGY AND THE CHANGING WORLD

THE GLOBAL VILLAGE

Periodically, technological change can be so dramatic that social studies and philosophy requires major revision. The Industrial Revolution certainly forced philosophers to re-think the categories of human experience and the recent information revolution is having a similar effect. The nature of human knowledge has been radically transformed by the new media technologies. The largely unregulated and uncontrollable Internet is seen by some philosophers to be a kind of microcosm of the postmodern world.

THE END OF HISTORY?

The so-called velvet revolutions of the late 1980s, which overturned Communism and eventually the Soviet Empire, had an enormous impact upon 20th century history. The most significant scholarly product of these revolutions was a book by Francis Fukhuama, an American academic who had also worked for the US state department. His book, *The End of History*, proclaimed the triumph of liberal capitalism and liberal democracy. Taking his inspiration from Hegel, Fukhuama claimed that the dialectical spirit of freedom

ABOVE: CZECH LEADER, VACLAV HAVEL, BECAME THE MOST ENIGMATIC FIGURE IN THE VELVET REVOLUTIONS WHICH SWEPT THROUGH EUROPE IN 1989.

CULTURAL DIFFERENCE

Traditionally, radical philosophy had been concerned with two issues, economic inequality and the ever-increasing power of the state. The conflicts which have emerged as a result of the new world order have forced philosophers to tackle new questions, most notably: which political system can best cope with cultural difference?

If the liberal democratic state is upheld by a philosophy which believed that cultural differences can always be reconciled, then how can we cope with a world where so many conflicts between cultural groups appear irreconcilable? Due to its descriptive rather than practical character, philosophy has tended to contribute to rather than resolve this problem.

THE FALL OF THE BERLIN WALL IN NOVEMBER 1989 RADICALLY CHANGED THE CULTURAL AND POLITICAL MAP OF EUROPE. THE EVENTS OF 1989 HAVE BECOME AS SIGNIFICANT FOR THE HISTORY OF HUMAN THOUGHT AS THE FRENCH REVOLUTION OF 1789.

which had driven human history was at an end. This, Fukhuama argued, had come about because the Western liberal democratic state was now the absolute realisation of the rational construction of human communities. *The End of History* has been ridiculed by the academic establishment, but its main argument is paralleled by certain tendencies within postmodern and radical philosophy. The discrediting of the idea of a universally just society has resulted in the disintegration of the revolutionary mindset. Consequently, the political imagination of contemporary philosophy has been less able to encompass concrete, practical and radical alternatives to liberal democracy.

THE NEW WORLD ORDER

The end of the Cold War brought significant changes in the global order. The bi-polar system of Capitalism versus Communism has been replaced by a new world order which is widely characterised as chaotic. The ideological void left by the collapse of the Cold War is now filled with more local expressions of social and political identity, such as nationalism and religious fanaticism.

JMAGO

ZEITSCHRIFT FÜR ANWENDUNG
DER PSYCHOANALYSE AUF DIE
GEISTESWISSENSCHAFTEN

HERAUSGEGEBEN VON
PROF. DR SIGM. FREUD

REDIGIERT VON
DR OTTO RANK U DR HANNS SACHS

1913
APRIL

1913

HUGO HELLER & Cle

PSYCHOANALYSIS AND PHILOSOPHY

The contribution of psychoanalysis to philosophy is a somewhat paradoxical one. It has taken philosophy in two quite different directions. On the one hand psychoanalysis presents itself as a science of the human mind. Practitioners of psychoanalysis can claim explanations for all forms of human behaviour. On the other hand, however, psychoanalysis champions a view of human beings which undermines the one which upheld the philosophy of the Enlightenment and thus scientific reason itself. In other words it also undermines the view, which found favour in the Enlightenment, that human beings are in essence autonomous rational agents who are masters of their own fate.

The picture of the human mind presented by the Austrian founder of psychoanalysis, Sigmund Freud, is one of a mind divided against itself, not more-or-less rational but more-or-less neurotic. For Freud, the mind is a well of psychic conflict between two competing forces. First there is the Id, which consists of instinctual desire. The Id conflicts with the superego, which is the part of the mind that reflects the social pressures of the norms and values of society and thus restricts the full realisation of the desires of the Id. The conflict between the Id and the superego is regulated by the ego, which concerns itself with reality – with how one's desires can be fulfilled or safeguarded. Consequently, the essential human condition is one of neurosis, whereby our desires struggle and often fail to find outlets. For Freud, one of the strongest causes of neurosis is sexual desire because our other instinctual desires, i.e. hunger etc, are more easily fulfilled. According to Freud, the

FREUD'S WORK REMAINS CONTROVERSIAL, PARTICULARLY HIS METHODOLOGY WHICH WAS BASED ON CONSULTATIONS WITH A SMALL SAMPLE OF WEALTHY MIDDLE-CLASS AUSTRIAN WOMEN.

repression of our sexuality can be traced to the Oedipus complex, which is the sexual relationship we develop with our parents. These desires are largely unconscious and of course unfulfilled, but the particular experience of each individual within this complex shapes his or her character.

Therefore, a great deal of psychoanalysis involves the explanation and interpretation of the unconscious.

THE UNCONSCIOUS

Psychoanalysis has always maintained a different status in philosophy than it has within its home discipline, psychology. Within mainstream psychology, Freud's work has been dismissed as unscientific and at best the idiosyncrasies of a man obsessed with sexuality. However, philosophy has to consider issues beyond those which concern the empirical explanation of human behaviour. In its pursuit of universal truths philosophy has to consider arguments and theories which may cause one to doubt the truth as it appears. If there is a realm of the mind called the unconscious, then there exists a powerful factor in our understanding of human existence which is prior to rationality and therefore beyond normal rational explanation. Consequently, Freud managed to generate considerable doubt about the progress of modern philosophy, through Descartes, Locke, Hume and Kant. However, because he was convinced that he had stumbled on a new science, he was less inclined to capitalise on the uncertainty which he had brought to the modern understanding of rationality. This has not been the case with many of the psychoanalysts who succeeded him. One of the most notable, recent philosophers who have attempted to develop Freud's revolutionary intervention into the understanding of human experience is the French philosopher, Jacques Lacan (1901–81). His work, which heralded a 'return to Freud', concentrated on the significance of the unconscious for human thought and attempted to demonstrate how the multiple networks of concepts, categories and symbols which go to make up our language are underpinned by the

Wien I. — Stubenring   N. Oes. Handels- und Gewerbekammer Stubenring 8910

IMPERIAL VIENNA WAS THE BIRTHPLACE OF PYSCHOANALYSIS. IT WAS HERE THAT FREUD CARRIED OUT HIS RESEARCH AND FORMULATED HIS THEORY OF CHILD DEVELOPMENT.

great abyss that is the unconscious. By challenging the idea that rationality has a transparent, objective status, Lacan also became an important figure of the postmodern movement in philosophy.

CIVILISATION AND ITS DISCONTENTS

Apart from radically altering the modern view of the formation of the human subject, psychoanalysis also effected perspectives on civilisation as a whole. It was Freud himself who initially broadened the scope of psychoanalysis. In his book, *Civilization and its Discontents*, he argued that all societies progress through the sublimation of instinctual desire. For Freud, the repression or control of instinctual desire is civilisation. The philosopher Herbert Marcuse summed up well the fatal paradox at the heart of Freud's work: 'The concept of man that emerges from Freudian theory is the most irrefutable indictment of Western civilization – and at the same time the most unshakeable defence of this civilization. According to Freud, the history of man is the history of repression…such constraint is the very precondition of progress.'

Philosophers such as Marcuse and others, including Michel Foucault, have taken Freudian theory and turned it on its head by using it as a basis for attacking Western Civilization.

Philosophy has long been intent on categorising human existence. By categorising the psychological, moral, cultural, national and international status of human beings, society could be organised accordingly. Even philosophies which claimed to be critical of the progress of Western societies participated in the further categorisation of human existence. Marx, for example, whilst critical of the atomistic, individualistic nature of capitalism, contributed to the categorisation of humanity by locating and cementing particular human identities, i.e. the proletariat and the bourgeoisie. The 20th century French thinker, Michel Foucault, was the first philosopher to understand this tendency and its consequences. His life and work were a struggle against it.

MICHEL FOUCAULT (1926–84)

TORTURED TEACHER

Foucault was born in Poitiers, France, in 1926, the son of wealthy parents. At the age of 20, Foucault entered the Ecole Normale Supérieure, a prestigious graduate school in Paris. It was in the highly competitive surroundings of the ENS that Foucault allegedly attempted to take his own life. If this is true, it confirms a self-destructive tendency in Foucault's character which revealed itself throughout his later life. Foucault published his first book, *Maladie Mentale et Personnalité*, whilst teaching psychology and philosophy at the University in Lille.

KNOWLEDGE AND POWER

Foucault looked to Friedrich Nietzsche, who had challenged traditional philosophy 100 years before, for inspiration. Nietzsche had substituted Kant's question, 'how is human knowledge possible?', for the question, 'why is human knowledge necessary?' His answer was that human knowledge is essentially a 'will to power'. Nietzsche argued that the quest for truth is driven by the desire to control and affirm human existence. Consequently, defining the truth is a matter of understanding our particular conceptions of truth, rather than what the truth actually is in a given circumstance. According to Nietzsche, no philosophy can define the truth without itself being caught up in a human will to power. Foucault follows Nietzsche in arguing that knowledge and power are therefore inseparable. Thus according to Foucault: 'Power and knowledge directly imply one another…there is no power relation without the correlative constitution of a field of knowledge, nor any knowledge that does not presuppose and constitute at the same time power relations.' According to Foucault, then, power is not merely a matter of the ability of A to persuade B to do what he otherwise might not. Consequently, power in society is not concentrated in the hands of those who control the coercive instruments of the state. This is because power is a positive as well as a negative force. The most crucial site of power is where force is unnecessary. It is where people willingly conform to social norms so that the use of physical force is made legitimate only when it is necessary. For Foucault, then, 'power in the west is what displays itself the most and thus hides itself the best'.

DISCIPLINE AND ORDER

Foucault's aim as a philosopher was to highlight hidden structures of power. The method he used was genealogy (from Nietzsche's *Genealogy of Morals*). This approach is a historical consideration of notions of truth and falsehood, good and evil, as they uphold power within society – for example, concepts of good and evil which underpin society's acceptance of the law.

One of Foucault's most powerful genealogies was his book *Discipline and Punish*. Foucault starts by describing a horrific 17th century public execution. This depiction illustrates a point of departure in the historic methods of punishment – from the highly visible public execution, where the focus of punishment was the body, to a less visible and more rationalised prison system, where the focus of punishment is the mind. This shift reflects the development of what Foucault calls the 'disciplinary society'. He employs Jeremy Bentham's model for a perfect Prison, the Panoptican. 'The theme of the Panoptican – supervision and observation, safety and knowledge, individualization and totalization, isolation and transparence – found the privileged site of its realization in the prison.' The way each prisoner is segmented in his cell and perpetually watched by guards from a central observation tower, whom he cannot see but is aware of, represents the new power created by the disciplinary society.

JEAN BAUDRILLARD
(1929–)

Born in Reims, France, in 1929, Baudrillard is one of the most enigmatic of all postmodern gurus. From 1966 to 1987, Baudrillard was Professor of Sociology at the University of Paris. During the 1980s he was one of the notorious, fashionable clan of Parisian intellectuals who attempted to push philosophy to breaking point and beyond. Baudrillard is most famous for the philosophy he built around the concept of 'hyperreality'. This term refers to the virtual or unreal nature of contemporary culture in an age of mass communication and mass consumption. Hyperreality was controversially applied to the Gulf War which, in the light of its coverage as a media event, Baudrillard proclaimed never actually happened. Apparently, his philosophical concern with the media and mass consumption led to the instalment of 50 television sets in his home.

THE DEATH OF SOCIETY

Baudrillard argues in his book *In the Shadow of the Silent Majorities* that contemporary society has entered into a phase of implosion. He says that the old structures of class have vanished into what he describes as the void of the masses: 'that spongy referent, that opaque but equally translucent reality, that nothing-ness: the masses'. The masses no longer make themselves evident as a class (a category which has lost its force because of a proliferation of possible identities), they have been swamped by so much meaning that they have lost all mean-

ABOVE: THE DOLLAR IS A CORNERSTONE OF AMERICAN LIFE. BAUDRILLARD'S PHILOSOPHY GIVES A VIVID INSIGHT INTO A SOCIETY DOMINATED BY MASS MEDIA, CONSUMPTION AND MONEY.

ing. They have been so continuously analysed through statistics, opinion polls and marketing that they do not respond to enlightened political representation. They have absorbed and neutralised ideology, religion and the transcendental aspirations that accompany them. The masses have also absorbed all the old, modern categories which were once a potentially liberating force. According to Baudrillard the 'law that is imposed on us is the law of confusion of categories. Everything is sexual. Everything is political. Everything is aesthetic. All at once...Each category is generalized to the greatest possible extent, so that it eventually loses all specificity and is reabsorbed by all other categories.'

HYPERREALITY

The 'massification' of society has led to the old forms of analysing society being abandoned. Baudrillard presents a new method of analysing society in his most famous book *America* which is written in the form of a travelogue. It provides an account of what Baudrillard believes is the unreality of American culture. His method was to travel through America at speed, not allowing enough time to become bogged down by the 'depth' of American social reality. He calls this method 'pure travelling' and says that in this way the banality of American culture can display itself. 'The point is not to write the sociology of the car, the point is to drive. That way you learn more about this society than all academia could ever tell you.' For Baudrillard America is a desert. It is a vast cultural void where the real and the unreal are merged so completely that distinctions between them disappear. People's whole lives are played out as if part of a film or soap opera. Despite appearances to the contrary Baudrillard is not making a moral judgement about contemporary culture, he does not intend to condemn it. In any case, for Baudrillard, the logic of good and evil is now so blurred that such an exercise is futile. The focus of much criticism directed at Baudrillard has been that human suffering is a very real feature of modern culture, but Baudrillard's position does nothing to alleviate it.

ABOVE: BAUDRILLARD BELIEVES THAT AMERICA IS SO ENGULFED IN THE IMAGERY OF ITS MASS MEDIA THAT THE LINES BETWEEN REALITY AND FICTION ARE BLURRED. THIS IS CLEARLY ILLUSTRATED BY PRESIDENTIAL ELECTION CAMPAIGNS.
BELOW: IN 1991 BAUDRILLARD FAMOUSLY PROCLAIMED THE GULF WAR NEVER REALLY HAPPENED.

THE POSTMODERN CONDITION

The Postmodern Condition was written as a report to the French government on the state of knowledge. Its central thesis is that the foundations of knowledge have been transformed from a modern to a postmodern condition. This transformation has radically altered the 'game rules of science, literature and the arts'.

The most distinctive feature of knowledge in the modern world was its search for universal and fixed answers to the great questions of human existence: who am I?, what can I know?, what ought I do? Those questions were answered through scientific rationality and political ideology in terms that left little room for exception to the universal rules they provided. Modern science affirmed that nature had a language which, if we could only

JEAN FRANÇOIS LYOTARD (1924–)

Jean François Lyotard was born in Versailles in 1924 and became one of the foremost postmodern philosophers. He is one of the few philosophers who have been able to give the term 'postmodern' an accessible and coherent meaning. Since 1952 Lyotard has taught philosophy in Algeria, Paris and California. His most famous book, *The Postmodern Condition*, written in 1984, sparked a fervent interest in his work which continues today.

ABOVE: COON'S WILLFUL ABANDONEMENT OF THE TRADITIONAL CATEGORIES OF ART, AESTHETICS AND MORALITY REFLECT THE KIND OF POSTMODERN ATTITUDE THAT LYOTARD DESCRIBES IN HIS BOOK *THE POSTMODERN CONDITION*.

speak it properly, would enable us totally to control our fate; nationalism persuaded us that the interests of every individual were best served by patriotism to the nation which had given him his being in the world. The list of attempts to realise a universal language for humanity is a long one. According to Lyotard, the distinctive feature of the postmodern world is a growing disrespect for these universal ideals. The first hints of disrespect can be traced to the late 1950s and 1960s, after Europe had begun to recover from the destruction of the Second World War. From this period onwards new conditions emerged which altered the state of knowledge in Western societies. The mass society (a product of the modern era) collapsed into one where human needs and desires were diversified. In this world according to Lyotard 'one listens to reggae, watches a western, eats McDonald's food for lunch and local cuisine for dinner, wears Paris perfume in Tokyo and retro clothes in Hong Kong; knowledge is a matter for TV games.' Through multiple media technologies, the voices of once oppressed identities, such as women and cultural or ethnic groups, found wider and more potent means of expression. In this new postmodern world, all the old economic boundaries of nation-states were eclipsed by global ones. With the result that the grand universal schemes of national political leaders and movements are redundant, powerless in the face of a global economy which is beyond their control. In philosophy and the human sciences, the idea that one could develop a scientific way of understanding society and human relationships within it is in tatters. The effect, in general, was to undermine all those universal hopes that had once gripped the modern world.

LANGUAGE GAMES

In contrast to the search for universal answers Lyotard offers a different way of understanding knowledge and its potential, one which is more in tune with the postmodern condition. In his book *The Differand*, Lyotard develops the idea that every particular cultural identity

LYOTARD BELIEVES THAT MEDIA INNOVATIONS, SUCH AS SATELLITE COMMUNICATIONS, HAVE CONTRIBUTED TO THE DEVELOPMENT OF A NEW ORDER IN WHICH NATIONAL POLITICS AND ECONOMIES ARE DWARFED BY NEW GLOBAL STRUCTURES.

can be understood as a language game. Within any particular language game there are rules and methods and common vocabularies which participants use to differentiate their own language game from others. Often, one language game will overlap with another or even be swallowed up by it. In this world of multiple, overlapping language games, no one particular language game has total control. Indeed, the differences between some language games can be so great that their rules render communication between them futile.

AN ECLECTIC THINKER

Derrida was born in Algeria in 1930 and moved to Paris in the 1950s where he joined a crop of radical intellectuals intent on tearing away the foundations of Western philosophy. His main intellectual ancestor is Heidegger, who also tried to break away from dominant traditions in philosophy. To a certain extent, Derrida achieved his aim by his disrespect for the traditional boundaries of philosophy. His work is eclectic and involves the disciplines of literary theory, sociology, psychoanalysis, art, linguistics and political theory. He has taught at Yale and John Hopkins University in America and is currently Directeur d'Études at the École des Hautes Études en Social Sciences in Paris.

THE WEST

Many of our most commonly held philosophical, political and cultural beliefs are bound by distinctions and dualisms. The most universal

JACQUES DERRIDA (1930–)

Jacques Derrida is one of the most important philosophers writing today. No other thinker has so radically and comprehensively questioned the entire Western philosophical tradition; and no other philosopher has as many disciples, interpreters and critics. Countless philosophers, mainly in North America and Europe, have dedicated their intellectual careers to interpreting and evaluating Derrida's work. Every book, article and interview he writes is pored over in the most minute detail. Derrida has transcended the status of a philosopher and is now a subject of study himself. This status is enhanced by Derrida's style of philosophy, which is full of idiosyncratic terminology and postmodern jargon which creates an interpretative uncertainty amongst commentators.

JOSEPH MCCARTHY'S ACCUSATIONS OF COMMUNIST INFILTRATION IN 1950S AMERICA CREATED PANIC IN THE WEST. FOR DERRIDA, MCCARTHY GAVE THE PERFECT EXAMPLE OF MYTHOS.

and political of these revolve around the concept of 'the West'. Placed at the centre of human civilization, the West is associated with values such as reason, progress, freedom and justice. The world outside the West is variously characterized by how far it is removed from these values. In opposition to the West are placed the values of superstition, despotism and irrationalism. For Jacques Derrida, the logic of this opposition goes all the way down to the most basic aspects of human identity. It can be found in the most inconspicuous of human values and the structure of the language we use to express them. It can also be found in the West's most celebrated novels, poetry and philosophy. Along with his philosophical mentor, Martin Heidegger, Derrida believes that the origins of this distinction can be traced to the Ancient Greek distinction between logos and mythos. For the Ancient Greeks, logos symbolised order and reason whilst mythos represented superstition and mystery. This distinction, which was preserved through Christian thought, became central to the identity of European culture, and therefore the West. According to Derrida, the distinction is so pervasive that it is internalized within our culture. The history of Western philosophy is, for Derrida, essentially a story of attempts to give this distinction more authority – to provide it with the stamp of certainty and truth.

task is more than an exercise in cultural history. Deconstruction entails highlighting how all the attempts to make the concepts of logos distinctive of western culture are informed by its opposite, mythos. He illustrates how the progress of reason and freedom in the West are explained by story telling, a quality normally associated with mythos. When western culture attempts to explain its history, it does so by employing the methods of the mythical story-teller. The rise of reason and freedom are given a heroic or tragic gloss, thereby contradicting the values of logos which it seeks to identify with. Derrida's method of deconstruction is useful for illustrating the ways in which racial identities are created. His disciples have provided interpretations of celebrated literature and shown how white Europeans are associated with all the values of logos, whilst others are associated with mythos. For this reason, Derrida is influential in English Literature departments, which in recent years have become interested in philosophy.

DECONSTRUCTION

The task that Derrida has set himself is to trace the dominance of logos (logo-centricism) within the culture of the West. He finds logo-centricism within, what he believes to be, the essential fabric of culture, language. However, the method which Derrida uses to do so, i.e. Deconstruction, indicates that this

LEFT: DERRIDA'S CONCERN FOR ISSUES OF CULTURAL IDENTITY ARE REFLECTED MOST POWERFULLY IN THE WEST'S CATEGORISATION OF THE ISLAMIC WORLD. THIS IDENTITY IS OFTEN INFORMED BY THE FANATICAL CHARACTERISTICS OF ISLAMIC FUNDAMENTALISM. UNTIL THE END OF THE COLD WAR, EASTERN EUROPE WAS REGARDED WITH SIMILAR DISTRUST.

RICHARD RORTY

In the 20th century philosophy has become a subject whose wisdom is for most of us out of reach. It is filled with strange and often meaningless jargon which when translated into layman's terms appears either to be irrelevant or obvious.

Philosophers are now specialists who rarely stray from their particular fields and rarely contribute to any wider public discussion about issues which can make a difference. Philosophy has of course always distanced itself from the rest of culture, but in recent years this distance has grown ever greater. The role which the philosopher once played as a kind of secular priest who could be called upon to resolve intellectual issues which couldn't be resolved elsewhere has been eclipsed by the growth of specialists whose authority in certain subjects is normally enough to satisfy demand for more accessible forms of wisdom. Whilst this has been happening however, popular interest in the great dead philosophers has increased, which suggests that there is no shortage of belief in the idea that philosophy can offer a special sort of wisdom.

TIME LINE

1931	Born in Chicago
1956	Rorty receives Doctorate at Yale
1979	Rorty is elected President of American Philosophical Association and his critically acclaimed work, *Philosophy and the Mirror of Nature* is published
1982	*Consequences of Pragmatism* is published
1989	*Contingency, Irony and Solidarity* is published

One philosopher, who recognises, and is willing to confront, the obscurity into which philosophy has fallen is Richard Rorty. As the author of some of the most controversial books in philosophy in the past 15-20 years, Rorty has in a sense blown the whistle on contemporary academic philosophy and as a consequence has felt the full force its scorn. He has, nonetheless, remained steadfast to his beliefs. There is, of course, nothing new about being sceptical of philosophy. One of Rorty's philosophical heroes, the American philosopher John Dewey, wrote nearly a century ago that philosophy had become out of reach to those outside the academy. However, few have managed to obtain the clarity of conviction and remedy that Rorty offers in this regard.

PHILOSOPHICAL THERAPY

For Rorty, the reason why philosophy has been led further into obscurity is that it has long reached a dead end in its quest to find certain knowledge or truth. On reaching this dead end it has sought to occupy itself with its own internal consistency, with concepts and ideas that it has invented to provide itself with foil for philosophical speculation. In *Philosophy and the Mirror of Nature*, Rorty states that the arguments philosophers have constructed for their philosophies of knowledge and truth are accidental rather than more-or-less objective. For Rorty, philosophy is simply one more 'voice in the conversation of mankind' which concentrates on one topic rather than any other because of other things happening elsewhere in the conversation, i.e. in science, politics or art. Every so often a philosopher of genius will create a philosophy so revolutionary that it throws the standard beliefs of philosophers into turmoil and thus manages to change the conversation. Such dramatic changes in the conversation are rare. Descartes managed it, as did Hegel, but mostly philosophers are gripped by the social norms of the particular conversation they are in. One of the tasks Rorty has set himself as a philosopher is to try and convince other philosophers that they are merely participants in one conversation amongst many others. By doing so Rorty sets himself up as a kind of therapist. His patients are philosophers who still believe that they have a certain kind of privileged knowledge. His method as a therapist is to attempt to get the patient to relive his past in order to cure him of 'the notion of the philosopher as knowing something about knowing which nobody else knows so well.'

Unsurprisingly many philosophers are unwilling to give up their privileged knowledge, which means that Rorty has to do more than force them to confront their past. He has to tackle the idea which keeps philosophy alive – the idea that there is a truth out there about the way the world is beneath all the

appearances. Rorty argues that truth simply isn't out there. Truth for Rorty is simply a condition of language. Essentially, truth is nothing more than what we agree upon as being true and what we agree as true is more a matter of social and historical circumstance than scientific or objective accuracy.

GLOSSARY

A priori knowledge: Knowledge which is prior to experience. In philosophy it is associated with the idea that the human mind contains innate properties which provide foundations for human rationality and understanding. However, *a priori* also refers to forms of justification in argument which do not depend on sensory or other kinds of experience. See Descartes and Kant.

Analytic/synthetic distinction: A theory of human judgement developed by Immanuel Kant which holds that propositions and judgements can be either analytic or synthetic. An analytic statement is one in which the predicate concept is contained in the subject concept, whilst for a synthetic statement the reverse is the case. The statement 'all bachelors are unmarried' is thus analytic and the statement 'all bachelors do not want to be married' is synthetic.

Being: A highly complex concept which has contained very different meanings in philosophy from the Ancient Greeks to the present day. Its most recent formulation was developed by Martin Heidegger. In his book *Being and Time* Heidegger argued that 'Being' precedes beings or objects because it constitutes the conditions in which those objects are understood and given meaning. For Heidegger, being is thoroughly historical and irreducible.

Cartesian dualism: The idea, developed by René Descartes, that the mind and body are two distinct realms which, despite their apparent incompatibility, somehow interact. This theory causes a number of problems, including: how can the physical and mental spheres connect?; are there universal natural laws which determine both spheres? is the world entirely mental?

Civil Society: The sphere of non-state institutions in which citizens, voluntarily or otherwise, participate in cultural and economic activities which shape their individual and collective identities other than those determined by the state. The concept of 'civil society' has proved to be particularly controversial in political philosophy, and views about its nature and function have been pivotal in the determination of particular philosophical schools. See Locke, Rousseau, Gramsci.

Communicative action: Currently very fashionable, the concept of communicative action has been developed by the contemporary German philosopher Jürgen Habermas. Put simply, it means action towards generating understanding and communication. This, for Habermas, is the primary political project of the modern world.

Deconstruction: A contemporary philosophical method, largely attributable to the work of Jacques Derrida, which is concerned with tracing the incoherence and contingency of philosophical arguments. A deconstructionist operates by playing off philosophical arguments against themselves.

Dialectics: A philosophy of logic which is sometimes extended to a view about the structure of the world and its development. The most famous dialectical philosophy was put forward by Hegel, whose holistic view of reality was guided by a view of human reason as a process of thesis, antithesis, synthesis.

Economic determinism: A crucial element of Marxist philosophy. Economic determinism is based upon the idea that all human history is determined by man's relationship to what he produces. Subsequently, no social, cultural or political phenomena can be explained outside of its economic significance. For example, nationalism and national identity can only be understood via their economic origins.

Empiricism: A school of philosophy which holds that knowledge is determined by sensory experience. See Locke, Berkeley, Hume.

Epistemology: The theory of knowledge. More specifically, the study of the limits and conditions of knowledge and justification.

Existentialism: A philosophical movement developed from the work of Kierkegaard, Heidegger and Sartre based upon the idea that each individual is his or her own world.

Falsification: A term used by Karl Popper to mark the boundaries between science and non-science. Popper argued that science progresses by means of the falsification of received scientific theories, which after vigorous examination are replaced by more persuasive ones. Theories that claim to be immune to eventual falsification are not scientific.

Humanism: A general perspective rather than a specific school of thought, humanism gives humanity and human beings a greater significance in the order of things than God or nature. The term only became fashionable in the 19th century but has been used to describe philosophy typical of the Renaissance.

Hyperreality: The idea that in a world where mass culture is dominated by mass media it has become difficult to distinguish between reality and fiction. In other words, the symbols and imagery of mass media have become so pervasive in contemporary culture that one can describe culture, at its most extreme in the United States, as 'hyperreal'. See Jean Baudrillard.

Idealism: A philosophical school which purports that reality is an entirely mental affair. In other words, objects which apparently have innate qualities separate from their conception in the mind are entirely mind-co-ordinated.

Inalienable rights: The idea, which became fashionable during the enlightenment, that human beings have certain fundamental, perhaps natural, rights which they cannot be denied. For example, the right to property, shelter, food etc. See Thomas Paine.

Language Games: A philosophy of language developed by the philosopher Ludwig Wittgenstein whereby language is understood as a complex network of overlapping games played by speakers. For Wittgenstein, every utterance is a move in a language game, which are more than linguistic practices, they are also forms of life. There is no universal rationality which underpins the rules of all language games, which means that philosophy itself is just a language game.

Logo-centricism: A term used by the philosopher Jacques Derrida to denote the centrality of logistic beliefs in Western culture.

Metaphysics: The philosophical examination of the nature and structure of reality. Unlike physics, metaphysics is concerned with the explanation of the extra/non-physical world, e.g. God, the human soul and the nature of space and time.

Paradigms: A concept developed by Thomas Kuhn in his attempt to delineate a philosophy of science. For Kuhn, science does not progress in a linear fashion, gradually moving closer to truth. Science is seen as being gripped, in any given period, by a dominant framework of values and beliefs (i.e. a paradigm) that sets criteria for assessing the credibility of any scientific claim, rather than having an objective criterion of truth.

Post-modernism: A philosophical movement which opposes those philosophies which it believes are typically modern, i.e. those centred around the European Enlightenment. It is, therefore, opposed to the idea that there can be a universal rationality or an objective theory of knowledge, or in general, that there can be permanent foundations of human knowledge. For most post-modern philosophers, human thought and knowledge is thoroughly historical and contingent.

Pragmatism: An essentially American philosophical school which originated in the 19th century. There are various schools of pragmatism but most pragmatists hold the basic argument that human knowledge is grounded in the contingencies of human evolution and human values/interests rather than rationality.

Totalitarianism: A highly controversial, social and political concept which, in the 1950's and 60's, became a fashionable way of describing the regimes of Stalin and Hitler. The definition given by Hannah Arendt remains the most cogent. For Arendt, totalitarian regimes are not merely dictatorships. Perhaps the outstanding characteristic of totalitarian regimes is the presence of total fear which pervades the lives of every human being.

INDEX

ACKNOWLEDGEMENTS

Picture research: Helen Fickling

The publisher would like to thank the following sources for their kind permission to reproduce the photographs in this book.

Ancient Art and Architecture Collection: 54 /55, 62 bottom

AKG London: 2/5, 7, 9 background, 27 bottom, 33, 36, 51, 59 64 top, 81 top, 95 left, 97 left, 102 bottom, 103, 104 bottom, 108, 109 top, 111 bottom, 126, 128 right, 140 top, 144, 150 background, 151 left, 152 background, 156, 159 right, 163, 164, 166, 168, 175 bottom; /Akademie der Bildenden Kuenste, Vienna 41 background; /Alte Pinakothek, Munich 40, 46 top right; /AP 39, 185 left; /Bibliotheque Nationale, Paris 24, 34; /Bibliotheque Nationale, Paris/Erich Lessing/ 74; /Musee Carnavalet/Erich Lessing/Paris 65; /Erich Lessing/Private Collection 45; /Erick Lessing/Hotel-Dieu Beaune 47 bottom left; /Schloss Ambras Collection, Innsbruck 142; /Erich Lessing/Gemaeldegalerie, Alte Meister, Dresden 22; /Kunsthistorisches Museum, Vienna/Erich Lessing 87; /Musee du Louvre, Paris 10 bottom left; /Erich Lessing/Musee du Louvre, Paris 12 bottom, 62 top; /Musee du Louvre, Paris 120 right, 141; /Sammlung Ludwig, AAchen 182; /Maximilianeum Collection, Munich 42; /Erich Lessing / Metropolitan Museum of Art, New York 17 top; /Museo del Prado, Madrid 81 bottom; /Erich Lessing/National Archaeological Museum, Athens 27 top; /Niedersaechsisches Landesmuseum, Hannover 61 bottom; /Peter Lothar 35 top left; /AP 181 bottom; /SMPK Nationalgalerie, Berlin 125 left; /Staatbibliothek, Berlin 25 background; /Tate Gallery, London 117; /Trinity College, Cambridge/ Erich Lessing 85; /Vatican Museums, Italy 8; /Fresco series in the Loggia/The Vatican, Italy 14 bottom; /Institut et Musee Voltaire, Geneva / Erich Lessing 75 right

Bridgeman Art Library: 105; /Musee des Beaux-Arts, Nantes/ Giraudon (Laboureur – Le Café du Commerce [detail]) 114 /115; /Bibliotheque Nationale, Paris 49 top right; /Bibliotheque Nationale, Paris/Giraudon 92; /Bonhams, London 118; /City of Bristol Museum and Art Gallery 161 top; /British Library, London 58 bottom; /Musee Carnavalet, Paris 101 left; /Musee de la Ville de Paris, Musee Carnavalet/Lauros-Giraudon 146,147 background; /Connaught Brown, London 180; /Museum of Fine Arts, Boston, Massachusetts 121; /Guildhall Art Gallery, Corporation of London 15 top; /Houses of Parliament, Westminster, London 99 right; /Kunsthistorisches Museum, Vienna 53; /Musee du Louvre, Paris/Peter Willi 64 bottom; /Musuee du Louvre, Paris/Peter Willi, 73 top; /Musee du Louvre, Paris/Lauros-Giraudon 84 bottom; /Metropolitan Museum of Art, New York 170,171 background; /Musee de Picardie Amiens, France 82; /Musee du Louvre, Paris / Giraudon 90, 91 background; /Museo Correr, Venice / Giraudon 75 left; /Museo d'Art di Ca Pesaro, Venice 179; /Museo di Goethe, Rome / Giraudon 79 right; /Museum of the City of New York 83 top; /National Gallery, London 23 centre right 72; /Philip Mould, Historical Portraits Ltd 153; /Private Collection 94, 99 left, 111 top,128 left, 133 top, 137, 148, 185 right; /Pushkin Museum, Moscow 23 top left; /Scottish National Portrait Gallery, Edinburgh 86 left; /Tate Gallery, London 1997.116; /Vatican Museums and Galleries, Rome 49 top left

Jean-Loup Charmet: 68, 76 background, 88, 107, 176 background

Corbis-Bettmann: 56 background, 63 bottom, 67 left, 119 B, 136 Bottom background, 139 bottom, 157 right, 167 bottom, 176, 178, 181 top; /Reuter 169, 173, 175 top; /Nik Wheeler 172 bottom; /Adam Woolfitt 165 bottom

E.T. Archive: 20 bottom, 71 background; /Civiche Racc d'art Pavia, Italy 13 top; /Gripsholm Castle, Sweden 70; /Victoria and Albert Museum, London 23 bottom left

Mary Evans Picture Library: 1, 10 background, 11, 14 top, 17 bottom, 19, 21, 28, 37, 38, 52, 56 bottom, 57, 69 top right, 77 top left, 93 top, 101 right, 102 top, 109 bottom, 127 bottom, 130, 131 background, 135 bottom, 139 top, 140 bottom, 143 bottom, 149 bottom, 151 right, 152 top, 157 left, 177, 186; /Sir WB Richmond 6; /Fawcett Library 155

Werner Forman Archive: 32 top, 123; /National Gallery Prague 30 background

Fotomas Index, London: 84 top, 134 background

Robert Harding Picture Library: /Advertasia Company Ltd 26; /Nigel Francis 32 background

Getty Images: 12 top background, 13 bottom, 15 bottom, 16 top, 18, 20 top, 29 top, 35 top right, 43, 44, 46 background, 47 top right, 48, 50, 58 top left, 60, 61 top, 63 top, 66 , 67 right, 69 bottom left, 73 bottom, 76 top left, 77 right, 78, 79 left, 83 bottom, 86 right, 93 bottom, 96, 97 right, 98, 100, 104 top, 106, 110, 113, 119 top, 120 left, 122 right, 124, 125 right, 127 top, 129, 133 bottom, 134 , 135 top, 136 top, 149 top, 154 , 158, 160, 161 bottom, 167 top, 172 top,184, 187 bottom

Image Bank: /Flip Chalfant 165 top

Image Select: 187 top; /Ann Ronan Collection/Image Select: 80, 95 right, 122 left, 159 left

Peter Newark's Pictures: 162

Ann & Bury Peerless: 29 bottom, 31

Science Photo Library: /GE Astro Space 183; /John Howard 143 top; /Nasa 174; /Alfred Pasieka 89

Sygma: /Keystone 112